SATANISM AND THE OCCULT

By the same author:

What is Love?
Secret Warriors
To God be the Glory
Close Encounters with the New Age
Paganism and the Occult

Satanism and the Occult

KEVIN LOGAN

KINGSWAY PUBLICATIONS

EASTBOURNE

ISBN 0 85476 479 8

Produced by Bookprint Creative Services
P.O. Box 827, BN21 3YJ, England, for
KINGSWAY PUBLICATIONS LTD
Lottbridge Drove, Eastbourne, E Sussex BN23 6NT.
Printed in Great Britain.

To Linda -
my better half and research partner.
To Peter and Cathryn,
and their future.

Contents

Acknowledgements

I am deeply indebted to many people for this book:

- to fellow Christian researchers, especially to Maureen Davies of the Beacon Foundation, who has contributed a chapter on her work caring for ritual abuse survivors, and to Patricia Hughes, who allowed me to use some of the findings of her Masters dissertation on satanic ritual abuse;
- to the policemen who watched over me in potentially dangerous situations, and those who assisted my investigations;
- to those who supported me in prayer throughout;
- to the dozen friendly critics who helped to hone my original manuscript into this finished product;
- to those in my home church and surrounding fellowships in East Lancashire, and elsewhere, who support me in ministry, and, most of all,
- to my family, who stand with me on the front line.

Foreword

In its increasing disllusionment with materialism, British society is steadily moving towards belief systems which appeal to feelings and intuition, sometimes at the expense of reason. This trend has helped to fuel a growing interest in the occult, including satanism, with the corresponding negative effects that brings to our society.

I have had the privilege of meeting the Reverend Kevin Logan, who is one of a small band of tireless campaigners doing their best to alert the church and society at large to the occult explosion occurring in our midst. Unlike the misleading stereotype of the 'hysterical and credulous evangelical' which some people like to propagate whenever a Christian speaks out on this issue, Kevin Logan is a level-headed, intelligent and caring vicar who is deeply concerned at the harm which the occult is causing to British society, and he is in a good position to know about this, having counselled many victims himself.

Sadly, despite years of warnings by activists such as Kevin Logan, the church appears ill-prepared to handle the occult explosion, and often resorts to indifference or denial as a response. The British government's attitude is no better. I believe this book will be a valuable contribution to the process of altering such views.

David Alton MP
May 1994

PART ONE

The Problem

1
The Questions
—by Way of Introduction

It is among people who think no evil that Evil can flourish without fear.

Logan Pearsall Smith.

Investigating satanism and the occult in the UK calls for the detection skills of a Morse or a Poirot. For a start, only a mere handful of our 55 million neighbours would openly accept such a description of their belief system. Secondly, they choose not to meet weekly at 10.30 on a Sunday morning with service noticeboards outside their churches, temples, lodges, grottoes, pylons or covens. For a mixture of reasons, they prefer a less public demonstration of their faith.

None of this helps to answer a dozen or more questions that are now being asked by an increasingly inquisitive public. Satanic and occult activities—whether on the stately estates of Princess Diana's brother[1] or in our criminal and family courts—continue to grab the headlines and our curiosity.

Does satanism really exist in our communities or just in the minds of Hollywood producers, tabloid newsmen and gullible Christians?

If satanists are out there, what are they like? How do they

operate? What do they believe and practise? Can anyone really worship Satan or is it just a good excuse for an orgy? How many satanists are there?

How do they fit in with others in the occult, like witches, pagans, druids and astrologers? Are they all the same as each other?

And if there really are black magicians, how can intelligent homo-sophisticated-sapiens march towards the third millennium with a creed dredged up from the Dark Ages?

Perhaps the biggest conundrum for the would-be detective on the trail of the occult is the satanic ritual abuse 'who-dun-it?'.

In a four-year period, nearly 130 children were tragically taken from their homes in the UK by officials following horrific allegations ranging from sexual abuse in rituals to human sacrifice. The police forces of Britain investigated a total of eighty-four separate cases of alleged ritual abuse.[2]

Are hoards of sex-mad satanists really to blame? Or is there a more prosaic explanation: over-zealous and over-imaginative social workers? Christian fundamentalists out to score points off the opposition? Over-ambitious therapists seeking to enhance reputations? Home-alone kids watching video nasties and losing touch with reality? What of the several hundred adults who have claimed to be ritually abused? Are they merely suffering from the latest psychological diagnosis—the False Memory Syndrome?

For the Christian, there are questions of a more religious nature concerning the satanic. As Christianity speeds further into a Decade of Evangelism, how on earth are we going to bring into the light the followers of the Prince of Darkness? Have we not enough on our plate without having to digest this unpalatable portion? And, is Satan massing his forces ready for the final conflict, or are we merely seeing too many red devils under the bed? And before all these are answered: is the Satan figure real or just a myth?

The answers to these and other questions will hopefully lead us to as much of the truth as anyone can know without actually becoming a satanist.

Truth and nothing but...

A word to you as the reader before we go further. As a group you will come from many walks of life.

First, to those of you who are among the million[3] or so in the occult, be you pagan, New Ager or satanist. You may fear that here is another Christian about to throw you to the lions of society. However, those of you who know my stance either through your journals, magazines and the media programmes or in personal conversations will, I hope, realise that I am not about to risk losing my soul—and yours—simply to gain worldly attention. My Lord takes a dim view of those who father lies.

To those in the occult who think they know me but don't, and have pigeon-holed me as an over-the-top fundamentalist, I ask for at least a fair hearing. What is set out in the following pages is the truth, as much of the whole truth as I know and, so help me, nothing but the truth.

Secondly, to fellow Christians. Some of you have tightly fixed opinions for, or against, satanism due to inherited fears, or perhaps recent fiascos such as Rochdale, or because of the blood-and-gore coverage of the subject in our tabloids. To you, I ask that you loosen your views a little and consider the latest evidence.

Other Christians may have feelings which rollercoaster between incredulity, voyeurism or even guilt at picking up a book on satanism. Perhaps before progressing, it might be good to settle your feelings before the Lord. Have a chat with him. Be honest. Do it now. The book can wait.

Thirdly, to those who are squeamish—Christian and non-Christian—the following pages will be hard. I have tried to eliminate the prurient, for no Christian writer wants to stir the dregs of human nature unless it is absolutely necessary to support and prove the arguments. If you find the going too much, please extract the general point I am making and move on to the next section. You may find this especially necessary in the first two chapters dealing with satanism and the occult on trial, and also the chapter on the shadow side of satanism.

To those Christians who are over-hardened to the realities of life: maybe this book will help to soften you—to feel, to pray and to act.

Fourthly, to those in the professions—the carers of all descriptions including psychiatrists, social workers and the police. The first eleven chapters of this book seek to set out a reasoned argument as to why you should take serious notice of the occult and its effects on those for whom you care.

I know that many of you are already persuaded because an increasing number of your "clients" have been adversely affected as satanism and the occult increasingly invade most levels of society. But others of you still fear that your professionalism may be put into question if you are seen to take on board satanism and the occult.

Why such a book?

There are seven good reasons for such a book as this at this time.

1. We need to identify, and learn how to cope with, the massive revolution in thinking that is well underway in our troubled land.

In recent decades, an encroaching worldview has been inducing us to bury our brains and live by our feelings. There is a growing belief that the old rational ways are responsible for our present mess, and that all we have left to rely on is our gut intuition. We, and everybody else, are being urged to do what we feel is right, according to our own eyes.

This follow-your-feelings world has been the cause of an explosion of interest in satanism and the occult and alternative spiritualities.

2. Satanism and the darker side of the occult are the eventual destination of a society which has lost touch with the old rational foundations and morals, many of which had their birth in our logical and reasonable Christian heritage. Despite our sophistication and technology, we are reverting to our old pre-Christian pagan ways.

3. Christians need to face these sad truths, accept the challenges they pose in this Decade of Evangelism and take on a multi-pagan world with the audacity and nerve that the first-century Christians demonstrated in a similar environment.

Good men and women need to be aware of what is happening in our land, so that they may promote the desirable and speak out against the evil. As Logan Pearsall Smith said, it is among people who think no evil that Evil can flourish without fear.

I hope this book will help us to face today's truths.

4. There is a great need to know the facts about the British scene after years of misleading, tragic and sometimes farcical headlines about satanism, child abuse and things that go bump in the night. This volume seeks to provide a corrective balance.

We need to understand the British scene for one major reason: there has been a massive satanic scare going on across the Atlantic, some of which we have experienced ourselves in places like Rochdale. Knowing the truth is important for ourselves, our nation and for the families and children who could be otherwise damaged.

5. It was time I committed to paper a decade of research and so provide various authorities with information which might assist them to take appropriate action.

A copy of the book has already been accepted and filed by the National Criminal Investigation Agency, a section of which has been gathering data on occult and satanic activities. Another copy was used by MP David Alton as he prepared his hugely successful campaign to persuade parliament to accept limits on the availability of video nasties.

6. As we prepared for printing, the controversy about satanic ritual abuse came to another of its peaks with the publication of two official reports. The first by the Metropolitan Police concluded that there was no evidence for a network of satanic abusers, and the second, produced by Professor Jean La Fontaine for the Department of Health, stated that, while there was small evidence of ritual abuse, there was no evidence of satanic ritual abuse in the eighty-four cases that had been investigated in Britain.[4]

Professor La Fontaine's report blamed the satanic ritual abuse scare on Evangelical Christians (out to prove that there was a real devil), aided and abetted by therapists, many of them untrained.

In between the publication of these two, came another entitled, *Treating Survivors of Satanist Abuse*, the work of thirty-eight eminent consultants, doctors and psychiatrists.[5] They reported that, far from being a myth, satanist abuse was an agonising reality both for them and the victims they treated regularly in their clinics.

As we went to print, it seemed that such a book as this could attempt to set a few records straight, and perhaps explain how such a massive contradiction could occur between respectable and professional pillars of society.

7. This book finally arises out of a decade spent ministering to those in the occult, and a yearning to save many I have come to know and love—even satanists!

Too often, our fear caricatures the enemy. We mentally adorn satanists, witches and the like with horns and barbed tails when in reality they can be caring, spiritually-hungry people. Certainly, I have felt the need to criticise their belief systems. And yes, I have posed hard searching questions for them in the following pages. But the main motivation is concern for those whom I believe to be lost.

This, incidentally, is another reason why I have sought to discover and present the truth, and nothing but the truth. The ministry of reaching and caring for those in the occult is hardly enhanced by the presentation of sensational half-truths and innuendo.

Black and white magic

I am forced to use 'black' and 'white' divisions of magic, even though they are a testing ground to determine whether or not a writer on occult matters knows what he is doing. For instance, the majority of witches and pagans refuse to acknowledge a 'black' or 'white' side to magic and condemn those who do as ignorant.

'Black magic doesn't exist as far as I'm concerned,' stressed Chris Bray, owner of the world's largest mail order occult company in Leeds. 'Magic is magic. It is ambient. We are all involved in magic by virtue of the fact that we exist. Everything that we do, every creative act, is an act of magic.'

A Blackpool chaos magician (one who uses any or all forms of magic that work for him) put it another way. 'Magic is neutral,' said Graham Fenn-Edwards, 'neither good nor bad; neither black nor white.' He likened magic to electricity which can warm or execute.

However, there are those in the occult like Beth Gurevitch, dressed head to toe in white, waving a star-tipped wand and claiming, 'I'm a white witch using my white magic for healing and for good.'[6] Though many in the occult dismiss her as little more than a television chat-show performer, she is not alone.

Other pagans plead to be known for their 'white magic', if only because the tabloid press—and therefore popular opinion— think in black-and-white, good-and-bad terms.

The satanist, on the other hand, boasts proudly of negotiating the darker Left Hand Path[7] of black magic and is contemptuous of those who disown it. One satanist temple divides its work between Greater and Lesser Black Magic.[8]

It is therefore difficult to write accurately about satanism unless a writer is free to use both terms.

2
Satanism and the Occult on Trial

The occult dictated the drugs and car-theft dealings of Jean Powell and Bernadette McNeilly...The evil chemistry between the two was spurred on by witchcraft and Stephen King horror books.[9]

'Paul was such a gentle boy,' explained his tearful grand-mother, Mrs Olive Weir.

Only minutes before, the judge had ordered her teenage grandson, Paul Bostock, to be detained in prison for an indefinite period. 'He was never in any trouble at work, at home or school,' added Mrs Weir. 'He wanted to be a policeman.'

Unknown to his family, this gentle boy had begun to fill the lonely hours of adolescence and youth with, among other things, the occult. After stabbing his first victim to death, he placed beside her torn body a piece of paper bearing a black magic symbol.

To say that the occult was the driving force behind the knife would be unforgivably simplistic. We human beings are a complex jigsaw cut by nature and nurture, and no one piece can fully do us justice. However, the prosecution in Bostock's case considered the occult to be highly significant and worthy of highlighting. Bostock had in fact plunged so far into the occult that he actually 'worshipped the devil'.

The jury at Leicester Crown Court was told that this was one of the influences which propelled Bostock as he committed his second murder while on his way to gloat over his first victim's grave. He was on the cemetery pathway when he attacked a young nurse, repeatedly stabbing her just as he had his first victim, a twenty-nine-year-old pet beautician who had been exercising her dogs.

Prosecuting QC David Farrer said of Bostock, 'It's plain that for years before then [the time of the murders], he had an unhealthy obsession with weapons, in particular knives, of which he maintained a collection at home. He also had an interest in horror, the occult and black magic.'

Because Bostock was under twenty-one, the judge could only order that he be detained in jail indefinitely.

If Paul Bostock and his occult-linked crimes stood in isolation, it would be sad but not unduly alarming. However, investigations reveal that it is far from unique in a decade interspersed with horrific occult and satanic-related crime. Our judicial system has sadly been one of the chief ways in which satanism and the occult have come to public attention. Bostock's crime, in June 1986, was one of the earliest in the decade I researched. It was by no means the last.

Black magic enthusiast Andrew Newell stabbed his flatmate to death in what the prosecution at Shrewsbury Crown Court in December 1987 called a ritual killing. Twenty-one-year-old Newell had stabbed twenty-year-old Philip Booth four times on what was claimed to be a makeshift black magic altar. Three of the wounds were to the heart, 'precise wounds likely to have been inflicted when the deceased was immobilised (held), rather than being inflicted in a stand-up fight', according to Special Bulletin No. 4O issued by West Mercia Constabulary Crime Information.

Timothy Barnes QC, prosecuting, said the 'sacrificial altar'

—a brown box—was in Newell's bedroom, and it was covered with bloody fingerprints and a huge smear of Booth's blood. When police examined the box, Newell pleaded with them not to open it, but they did and found a record case containing black magic books, a white-handled knife, candles and an altar cloth. There was also an inverted cross drawn in human blood and the names 'Lucifer' and 'Satan'. The following satanic poem was found among the occult paraphernalia:

> Torches blazed and scorched.
> Children were burned as they started to cry,
> Hands held in the sky.
> In the night fires burning bright.
> The ritual has begun.
> Satan's work is done.

The sentence, '666, the number of the beast, sacrifice is going on tonight,' was written next to the poem.[10] Around the room were found references in Newell's handwriting to witches and warlocks. There was also a letter addressed to a leading occult British mail order company in which Newell asked for help, stating that he wanted 'to go further and reap the benefits of the occult'. He was sentenced to life imprisonment for murder, though this was later reduced at appeal to the charge of manslaughter.

One of the distressing features of my research on a decade of occult-related crime is the seemingly inevitable involvement of the young.

In a year when 75,000 youngsters ran away (1988)[11]—many hoping for freedom and fortune in our big-city streets—a young teenage girl absconded from a suburban children's home and arrived penniless in London. She thought fortune had smiled on her when mother-of-three Hazel Paul took her into her home in Gladesmore Road, Tottenham. It hadn't. There was to be nothing fortunate about the meeting, and she was also to lose her freedom for six terrifying days.

An Old Bailey jury was told that the young girl was held against her will and tortured during 'bizarre black magic sessions'. Helping Paul were seventeen-year-old Loretta Henry and a fifteen-year-old boy, both of whom claimed that Paul had coerced them with her 'psychic powers'.

'I was just doing things Hazel told me,' said the boy. 'I was not stopping to think. It was weird.'

Judge Peter Mason QC, sentencing Paul to five years for false imprisonment and causing grievous bodily harm, said, 'Any right-thinking person must have been horrified at the account given in this court.' Henry was jailed for eighteen months and the boy given two years' detention for ill-treating the girl on Paul's instructions.

During the runaway's 'imprisonment', she was forced to endure ouija board sessions in which the devil was invoked. On one such occasion the girl had been ordered to strip naked and she began to behave in a peculiar manner.

'I asked Hazel why the girl was making these breathing noises,' the boy said in evidence. 'Hazel said the devil was having sexual intercourse with her. I was really frightened.'

At other times, the girl's hands and feet were hit repeatedly with a hammer and she was cut on the arms and legs with a hacksaw and an electric carving knife. The horrific events had been sparked off when the girl was accused of stealing money from a gas meter. This young victim was fortunate compared to the tragic Suzanne Capper, who died after a week of similar torture in what a police spokesman described as a murder 'foul and evil beyond belief'.

Manchester Crown Court heard in December 1993 how two women and two men tied sixteen-year-old Suzanne to a bed for six days, beat her and tortured her, brainwashed her with chants from the occult horror film *Child's Play*, pumped her full of drugs, pulled out her teeth and finally dumped her in the country, dowsing her with petrol and turning her into a human torch. Incredibly, she survived long enough to crawl for help, and to tell the police her appalling story.

Subsequently, Bernadette McNeilly, Jean Powell, Glyn Powell and Anthony Dudson were found guilty of what Mr Justice Potts said was 'as appalling a murder as it is possible to imagine'. The four were jailed for life.

The day after the sentencing, the newspaper headlines revealed: 'Occult fuelled evil empire' and, 'Ritual torture in the witches' den'. The reports explained how two women governed by their occult interests led a small gang of petty criminals. *Today* newspaper explained: 'The occult dictated the drugs and car-theft dealings of Jean Powell and Bernadette McNeilly. Sex-mad Berni read the gang's fortunes by throwing rune stones. If the omens were unclear there were always the tarot cards…the evil chemistry between the two was spurred on by witchcraft and Stephen King horror books.'

McNeilly was said to be 'obsessed' with Chucky, the doll in the *Child's Play* video series, said in the stories to be inhabited by the soul of a dead strangler.

This was an echo of the Jamie Bulger murder a few weeks prior to the Capper case. The third video in the *Child's Play* series was known to have been in the house of one of the two ten-year-olds who killed Jamie, though it was not proved that either boy had seen it. However, in *Child's Play 3*, Chucky was spattered with blue paint—so too was Jamie. The doll was badly mutilated—so too was Jamie. Chucky the doll died beside a railway track—so too did Jamie. The trial judge ordered the two boys to be detained at Her Majesty's pleasure and stated his personal belief that the occult horror videos had played a significant role in inspiring the killers' behaviour.

It is difficult to write about such actions, and just as hard to read and digest. Yet it is necessary to go into at least the basic facts so that we might remind ourselves of what is actually happening today in our so-called sophisticated society.

By way of a reminder, feel free to pass on to Chapter 4 at any time you wish, though hopefully not before accepting the sad link between the occult and crime, and how these, and subsequent, reports have focused public attention on the occult and the satanic.

The occult defence

Justice demands that the accused be given the right to a defence, and so we must include from the start of our thinking the comments of those in the occult. Their views came to light as I and others began to voice our fears about the occult influence on society at the turn of the present decade. Taking a courageous lead in this were groups like the Evangelical Alliance, Reachout Trust, Cult Information Centre and the Christian Response to the Occult (CRO) and the Beacon Foundation[12]. Press and television gave their warnings about the occult dangers headline treatment, and soon journalists were demanding more and more evidence for our concerns. At this time, I was able to release the early findings of my research into occult-related crime.

Even as this was done, I was conscious that it is all too easy to demonise a group of people by creating a false monster image around them. However, my task was not to blacken reputations unjustly, but rather to point out that there was, at the very least, a case to answer because of the increasing occult and satanic-related problems arising in society, and especially in the courts.

When some of the occult-related crime cases were made public, leading British occultists promptly attacked them as inaccurate. One such defence advocate was Chris Bray who, believing that the occult required a champion, launched his

Sorcerer's Apprentice Fighting Fund (SAFF)—later renamed the Sub-culture Alternatives Freedom Foundation. One of the SAFF leaflets claimed to set out 'the truths' of the cases as opposed to my 'tales'.[13] This accepted that all the court cases I had cited were authentic, but attempted to give alternative explanations to disprove occult connections. However, the leaflets claim to show the 'truths' was actually a long way short of doing so.[14]

To ensure fairness and accuracy, Linda (my wife and research partner) and I visited the Sorcerer's Apprentice to interview Mr Bray about his defence of the occult, among other things.

Asked about a decade of occult-related crimes, he replied: 'Every case that has been produced in every book so far, we have been able to undermine by the truth. When I say undermine, what I am saying is, we are looking at the qualifications that people like yourself say are occult which signify satanism. We're saying that that's not how occultism and satanism work. Occultists and satanists don't do that sort of thing. The mere fact that you have an incense burner or black candles does not mean that you are a satanist. Now, I'm not sticking my head in the sand and saying that somewhere in the world there isn't a paedophile who is at some time or other going to try and use occultism as their *modus operandi*. But that's not satanism either. That's a paedophile using the occult as a front, just as in the same way they use the Boy Scouts as a front.'

Mr Bray's main argument was summed up a little later when he claimed that those 'seriously involved in occultism' were not involved in crime. To suggest that they were would be a 'contradiction in terms'. A person could not be an occultist and a criminal.

This begs two important questions:

1. The Sorcerer's Apprentice sells tapes and books which often acknowledge that the way of the occultist is dangerous and can lead to loss of control.[15]

The occult cannot have it both ways. It cannot call people occultists when they behave themselves and then disown them when the occultism leads them to lose control and kill or torture.

2. The occult must also answer the serious charge of leading many up a weird maze of conflicting paths. For instance, few in the occult can agree on what magic is, let alone how to control it. The name and nature of the force involves changes from coven to coven and, as we shall read later, one group of occultists are often anxious to rubbish the claims of fellow occultists. Those who follow the so-called good Right Hand Path criticise those treading the dark Left Hand Path and vice versa. One supplier sues another for libel. On top of all this, there are no generally acknowledged rights or wrongs; no great ethical guidelines; everybody has their own 'Ten Commandments'. Aleister Crowley, the leading occultist of this century, simply ruled: 'Do what thou wilt shall be the whole law.'

Bearing all this in mind, consider the plight of the naive, susceptible occult youngster who descends into this dangerous underworld of internecine warfare. Is it any wonder he ends up confused and out of control, adrift from right and wrong and not knowing which way to turn?

We see this with increasing clarity as we continue to examine our case histories. Again we note how it is often the young who suffer the most.

Suicides

Two girls existed for a decade with the constant nightmare that their parents would kill themselves as part of some bizarre occult ritual. A Scarborough inquest was told in April 1993 of how former army Warrant Officer Barry Pexton, forty-five, and his thirty-eight-year-old wife Carol committed suicide in a fume-filled car because they were on an occult mission to get to the other side and, ironically, 'battle against evil'.

The elder daughter told the jury, 'We had always been told there was a possibility that they would commit suicide. We had been conditioned over a period of ten years to know exactly what to do and what to say.'

Suicides form one of the largest groups in occult-related court cases, and I suggest that that is no coincidence. Any susceptible youngster or adult caught in a confusion of occult contradictions is unlikely to find much comfort. The Office of Population Censuses and Surveys showed in July 1993 that the number of men who commit suicide (4,362 for that year) had risen by more than a quarter in the previous decade. The increase was most marked in the fifteen to forty-four age group.

Two of these cold statistics represented Essex bank clerks Ian Swanson, twenty, and Iain Davidson, eighteen. They were involved in fantasy role-playing games of death and black magic. Magazines detailing how to play the games were found alongside their bodies in a fume-filled Ford Capri, a Southend inquest heard in February 1993.

The same national survey which revealed increases in male suicides also showed that the number of female suicides dropped by 32% over the same period. Samaritans suggested that the 'increased degree of self-worth' given to women by modern society was the likeliest reason. This, however, was not true for one sad woman who took her own life, in what was a tragic sequel to a rather strange incident recorded in my earlier book, *Paganism and the Occult*.[16] The facts were these:

A traffic patrolman signalled for the speeding lady driver to pull over. The events which followed put the police force of a large northern town on full alert for a missing officer. The police driver asked for her documents, but the woman explained with a pleasant smile that they were at her home nearby. She invited him to follow her, and the officer took the unusual course of agreeing.[17] After a short run, the woman turned down a narrow lane, and then into the driveway leading to a large ranch-type bungalow. As the police officer followed, he saw two notices declaring: 'NO ENTRY – Trespassers will be prosecuted'.

Two things made him slow down as he came to the entrance. The first was the knowledge that the bungalow was situated in the town's radio 'black spot' and he had failed to report where he was going. The second was the sight of strange mythological beasts and demonic gargoyles which surrounded and surmounted the gateway.

Drawing to a halt, he recollected an investigation which one of his colleagues had conducted some weeks before. It had been something to do with a young girl being held against her will on a secluded stud farm, and there had been mention of witchcraft and drugs. This, he now recalled, was the same place. He had laughed when told about the 'devil group with lots of surplus young girls hanging around'. Now, he was not too amused as he stepped from his car beneath a large CB aerial flying a strange flag with a gold five-pointed star (an occult symbol).[18]

By this time the woman had left the car and the officer followed her into the house. He noticed a picture of a furry creature with a goat's head and cloven hooves as they entered the sitting room.

'That's a bit ghoulish,' he joked nervously. 'Is it the devil?' The woman's strange reaction completely unnerved him.

'Her eyes began to roll and then the pupils disappeared upwards,' he later told his superiors. 'She began to make weird, inhuman sounds and went as stiff as a board. And then the picture itself seemed to come alive.'

This proved too much for the officer and he decided to make an excuse and leave. He did so quickly, but went into the wrong room which was full of 'weird things'.

'I lost my bottle completely and ran,' he explained later. It was two hours before he felt sufficiently recovered to stop at a phone box and report in.

A short while after the alert had been called off for the missing officer, a CID friend contacted me to see if I could help with their enquiries. Apparently, people connected with the ranch bungalow were suspected of being involved in the exhumation of bodies at two nearby churches when skulls and other bones had been removed, and also the disappearance of three goats on or about the thirteenth of each of the previous three months.

That was the story in 1988. Five years later the tragic sequel hit the headlines when one of the female residents of the bungalow took a fatal overdose of tablets. For legal reasons which prevent me from identifying the suicide with the first story, I am unable to use the woman's name. Her mother told the inquest that her daughter became involved in witchcraft when she went to work at the stud farm. Her personality 'changed dramatically' and she then sent home a note stating, 'I renounce all forms of God and take Lucifer as my God.'

As I write, the mother is pursuing her grievances through the civil courts against the new owners of the ranch bungalow. She gave her daughter the money to buy the property, only to discover that she had been influenced to sign over the deeds to the group leader.

Grave robbers or glue sniffers?

The second largest section in my list of occult-related crimes is perhaps the most unsatisfactory. There are few convictions and much that is inconclusive or merely circumstantial. It is the long list of grave robberies and church/cemetery desecrations.

In my first list of occult-related crimes, one involved Brookwood, the nation's biggest cemetery, which is raided on average about a dozen times a year. One such incident resulted in the conviction in May 1987 of Shane Tonks, twenty, of Farnborough who was fined £150 for carrying off a severed head. The SAFF 'Truth' article pointed out, quite rightly, that there could be numerous explanations.

'There was no proven occult connection in this case,' stated the article. 'Police files show that the most usual motivation for vandalism of graves is a bet or dare. Glue sniffers notoriously frequent cemeteries. Archeologists make a profession from rifling graves. If satanists are supposed to resort to human sacrifice so readily why would they need to dig up someone already dead?'

Good points, except perhaps for the last two. I find it hard to visualise too many archeologists snatching bodies in the 1990s from quaint English churchyards in the dead of night. And there are, as SAFF writers know well, satanic and occult rituals which call for human remains, notably concerned with necromancy ('the calling back into temporary "life" the spirit of a corpse, in order to persuade it to give information about the past and the future').[19]

Necromancy was certainly suspected in Coppull, Lancashire, in 1990 where a body was disinterred and then apparently used in some form of ritual. It was the second time it had happened in that particular churchyard. However, the points about vandalism and glue-sniffers need to be borne in mind.

These causes, however, were not the first considerations for mid-Devon police who investigated the fire which gutted Buckfastleigh's famous 'Hound of the Baskerville' parish church in July 1992.

Fiction had long linked the church with Satan ever since Sherlock Holmes set off from Baker Street for the wilds of Dartmoor to tackle the Hound of the Baskervilles. Conan Doyle has him saying to Watson, "Yes, the setting is a worthy one. If the devil did desire to have a hand in the affairs of men...."

The 3,700 inhabitants of Buckfastleigh, together with the police and the local vicar, now think it likely that the link is no longer pure fiction. It was known that a satanist-type group had broken into the church several months before the fire and conducted some form of ritual on or near the altar. The fire apparently had started in this area. Yes, it could have been vandals or glue-sniffers, but the people of Buckfastleigh do not think the possibility of devil-worshippers should be lightly dismissed.

Nor do Isle of Wight police, who continue their search as I write for what the RSPCA believed to be devil-worshippers sacrificing several pet rabbits, desecrating graves with crosses on them and what looked like the ritual killing of a goat. Inspector Steve Evans of Ryde police said, 'These are sickening incidents and one wonders at the state of mind of the perpetrators.'

The occult and madness

Let us return to the safer ground of the proven—the criminal courts. Yet, as we do so, we address one area of research which raises an important question. It is the difficult chicken-and-egg query of which came first—mental illness or the occult. When a person commits an occult-related crime and is sent to a mental asylum rather than prison, did she (more often 'she' than 'he' in these cases) commit the crime and get into the occult because of her illness, or did her involvement with the occult bring on the illness that made her then commit the crime?

Take, for instance, twenty-year-old Tracey Barrett of Langley, Berks. Reading Crown Court was told in December 1992 that she had taken part in the 'bizarre ritual killing' of Ian Clarke, fifty-nine, who was a loner interested in the occult. She was sent to Broadmoor.

A second case concerns twenty-three-year-old Sheena McLaughlin who tried to strangle her three-month-old daughter because her spirit guide told her: 'Your child has to die.' Her life was 'ruled by the occult and tarot cards', Glasgow Crown court heard in January 1986. The judge accepted her plea of guilty to culpable homicide on the grounds of diminished responsibility.

Just what was the main influence on these women's lives: mental illness or strange occult beliefs? The available information on Tracey's case would indicate that an unhinged mind caused her to act murderously. The occult was incidental. However, in Sheena's case there is a possibility, perhaps even a probability, that the occult was formative. It is the experience of most of those who deal with those lost in the occult, that responsible action is all too easily diminished when young, susceptible people are caught in a web of spirit guides, tarot cards and bizarre occult rituals.

Sheena's accomplice, self-acclaimed spiritualist and occultist Alan Porter, was certainly not suffering from an impaired mind. He knew exactly what he was doing when he finished off the grisly task that Sheena had started. He was sentenced to life imprisonment for killing her daughter.

Occultists or paedophiles?

A small number of occult-related crimes beg a different question. Does the occult inspire the crime or are the perpetrators merely using the occult to aid their crime? Nowhere is this more pointed than in the area of child abuse. Do the guilty abuse as part of the occult or because they are inspired by the occult, or are they simply paedophiles using the occult as just another 'frightener' to keep their victims quiet?

The occult certainly seemed to be involved at the heart of obscene rituals inflicted by Brian Williams, of East London, on two sixteen-year-old girls. It was the same when he compelled fifteen other youngsters to submit to black magic rites. He convinced them that he was the devil and forced some of them to cut themselves before making them draw occult symbols in their own blood and indulge in indecent acts.

But after the case had been dealt with, occult leaders claimed that Williams was only using the 'devil talk' to scare the kids into obeying his evil commands. It is possible. I'm not convinced myself, but I have to admit that it is possible. The judge jailed him for eleven years in July 1987.

There was another abuse case where occult leaders claimed that their beliefs were being falsely used by a paedophile. But this time I believe that they were definitely wrong.

A thirty-eight-year-old Hemel Hempstead man was dubbed by the press as 'the most evil man in Britain'. Peter McKenzie was a self-styled wizard who lured into a web of sex and debauchery thirteen young girls, some as young as six. In his 'magic circle', he promised his victims that they could become witches with special powers, providing that they indulged in sexual acts with him. He warned the children that if they ever told their parents, bad luck would befall them and they might even die. McKenzie used his first victim, the seven-year-old daughter of a woman friend, to recruit others. The girl innocently brought her schoolfriends to McKenzie who then gave each a wand. He taught the first girl to pray nightly to the god 'of lechery and debauchery', Asmodeus, and made her swear to silence.

Chris Bray, in his defence of the occult, regarded this particular case as a classic example of a paedophile using and abusing the occult. He said it was also an example of how the prosecution used and abused the occult simply to gain the jury's sympathy, and thus secure a conviction.

But Mr Bray got his facts wrong.

He explained to my wife and me during a tape-recorded interview: 'It wasn't abuse in a satanic ritual. The names that he [McKenzie] used to try and convince the girls that he was involved in magic were not proper occult names...like, for instance, Abaddon, who is a prince of knowledge who searches out treasure...when you get all these facts together something doesn't click.'

What doesn't click is Mr Bray's information. McKenzie did not use 'Abaddon' but 'Asmodeus'—and Asmodeus is certainly the one with 'the power of the deadly sin of lechery', according to the occultists' own encylopedias.[20]

This showed McKenzie indeed knew what he was talking about. It means that he was not simply using the occult as a 'frightener'. It was a subject in which he was extremely well versed and practised.

It is interesting to note that Chris Bray was one of Professor La Fonataine's 'helpers' when she produced her Government report stating that there was no evidence of satanic ritual abuse. Mr Bray has 'indefatigable in sending me material,' she says in the report's acknowledgements.

Let lie on file

This legal ruling allows charges to be kept on file for future use, if necessary. The prosecution, for instance, allows a charge to lie on file when there is more than sufficient evidence to ensure a conviction.

Lack of space means that scores of other occult-inspired crimes lie unused in my research file. There is no room to deal with the Oxford schoolboy hooked on occult horror videos who shot two teachers and a pupil, nor the Norwich clairvoyant who 'cynically' fleeced a despairing wife claiming to cast spells over her husband, nor self-confessed satanist Derry Mainwaring Knight who received a seven-year jail sentence for obtaining more than £200,000 by deception, nor a hundred and one other similar incidents.

We need also to bear in mind that only a minority of occult-related cases reach the public. The others either remain unknown, as with much unreported or undetected crime in the land, or they come before the courts with little or no reference to their occult links. One medium-ranking police officer had cause to ask other colleagues for any information they had of any occult-related crimes. The officer was amazed at the response.

'This is going on all over the country,' the officer said, 'and it goes largely unnoticed because nobody in the force is collating it. There are no official statistics about occult-related crime because no such category exists on the computer.'

It would be wrong, however, to let one category of crime— the biggest in my research file—lie unattended and unaddressed. For this is the crime which has brought the occult in general, and satanism in particular, to the public's attention in the last five years: ritual abuse.

This crime not only has the occult community firing all its big guns in defence, but there is also an unhealthy crossfire from many parts of the media and the establishment who maintain that the ritual abuse of the last few years has merely been one huge tragic hoax; a ritual fabrication.

The evidence now available shows that they are almost certainly right in some cases—and possibly, even probably, wrong in others.

3
On Trial (Part Two)

Your fascination with the occult and devil worship played a part in impelling you towards this evil behaviour.[21]

It was not exactly a dawn raid but it felt like it for Veronica[22] and her two sleepy-eyed children. Daylight had streaked the sky a full two hours before the noise and knocking at 7 o'clock on that fateful summer morning in 1990. Save for that, in all other respects it felt like a dawn raid. The terror was present. So too were the stony official faces. Worst of all was the sudden suffocating impotence of the state taking over each and every decision of family life.

Veronica could not know it then, but it was to be a long agonising year before she and the children would once again be together in their own home.

Veronica and sixteen other Liverpool adults—including preachers, company directors, a teacher and an education official were rounded up by ninety-seven police officers, with fifteen social workers on hand to take into care eight children aged between six and fifteen.

Covert investigations had begun as early as the previous Christmas following allegations of child abuse and devil worship from two teenage children already in care. Following the synchronised raids, one police officer, questioned by reporters about rumours of foetuses being used in satanic ritual, said, 'We may have to dig up gardens.'

By the time of this raid, 'ritual abuse' had become a normal working phrase for those like myself involved in supporting victims. But for society as a whole, it was still a mysterious phrase and, not unreasonably, there were growing demands for more evidence, despite the much-quoted Nottingham abuse case in 1989. Nottingham (dealt with later in this chapter) had, however, been constantly criticised when categorised as a ritual abuse case, and an increasing number of concerned professionals were beginning to hope for a court verdict that would put this type of crime beyond dispute. Consequently, the emotions of many in the caring professions were caught in an uncomfortable yo-yo: up one moment, hoping for proof and therefore vindication for their clients or charges and themselves; down the next, yearning for the whole dirty nightmare to dissolve away.

Within hours of the round-up operation in Liverpool, the original stories given by the abused girls were beginning to dissolve into exactly what they were—silly, vindictive tales of two unhappy adolescents. I, among others, was to spend much of the following year helping Veronica to retain her sanity while supporting her in her fight for the return of her children.

Liverpool was closely followed by Rochdale and the Orkneys, and the ensuing explosion of a thousand and one views around the controversial crime created the extraordinary emotional backlash that effectively jammed the lid on the whole issue. Suddenly, talk of ritual abuse became offensive and unwanted in the public arena. The establishment—inescapably in the hysteria—added its own slow-moving, bureaucratic weight to the lid by announcing a two-year enquiry.[23]

The backlash against ritual abuse provides a fascinating but disturbing insight into how humans face the inhuman. Here are some common reactions:

'This sort of thing just doesn't happen in modern society.'

'It may happen somewhere, but not in our county/town village/street.'

'It's crazy; all in the minds of video-mad kids/unbelievable social workers/fundamentalist Christians.[24]

In addition to the obstacle of incredulity, there was the understandable query about what was involved. One television journalist interviewing me put it this way: 'What do you want me to accept; what are we talking about? Ritual? What sort of ritual? Who is doing what to whom? And why?'

There is no one widely accepted definition of ritual abuse hardly surprising considering the controversial nature of the issue. However, definitions used by child agencies and police in England, Canada, Holland, Australia and the USA comprise most, if not all, of the following elements:[25]

* Ritual abuse involves children, adolescents and/or adults.
* The abuse is physical, sexual, emotional and/or psychological.
* It is performed in a context linked with symbols or activities that have religious, magical or supernatural connotations.
* It is not always satanic, but many survivors speak of involvement with some form of satanism.
* The symbols or activities, repeated often over time, are used to frighten and intimidate victims or to convert them to perpetrators' beliefs.

Note that some agencies, like the NSPCC, prefer to use 'ritualistic abuse' which is grammatically more accurate than 'ritual abuse', but the latter term is employed throughout this book because it is in common usage.

The British cases of satanism and ritual abuse have fallen

into four general categories: the impossible, the possible, the probable, and the positive.

The impossible

Had the phrase 'satanic ritual abuse' never entered the social care vocabulary, the cases in this category might never have happened, or if they had, they would hardly have caused a ripple on the surface of public opinion.

Returning to the story of Veronica, by way of example, the facts were these: two teenage girls were taken into care and began to disclose to social workers how the pastor of their Pentecostal fellowship, together with other leaders and members, had abused them and several other children in satanic rituals inside the church. The teenagers mentioned the sacrifices of animals and children, and they had started to name names. The disclosing teenagers came from a broken home and had themselves been emotionally and physically abused.

By this time, New Year 1990, satanic ritual abuse had become the latest social phenomenon in professional carers' circles, with extensive reports appearing in magazines such as *Social Work Today* and *Community Care—The Independent Voice of Social Work*.[26] They encouraged carers to 'face the unbelievable', and discussed care issues raised by children abused in 'sex rings and satanic cults'. Halfway through the investigation came further encouragement via the annual report of the National Society for the Prevention of Cruelty to Children, and the claim that up to nine of its sixty-six area teams had dealt with ritual abuse cases.[27]

In consultation with the police, social workers from Liverpool and nearby Knowsley, eventually decided to act on the teenagers' testimony. In the ensuing home raids, searches and interrogations, the required supporting evidence would hopefully surface and care orders and prosecutions could safely follow.

Within days, it was obvious that there was no such supporting evidence and the adults, including Veronica, were released—but not her two children. Police and social workers had found copies of personal letters mentioning Veronica's battle to be free of the pagan-witchcraft religion of Wicca in which she had been involved, and her subsequent conversion to Christianity two years prior.

I have to admit that had I been a social worker faced with this evidence, not to mention the then prevailing climate of opinion, I too might have kept the children in care pending further enquiries. What I would not have done, I hope, was to stretch out those enquiries month after month—for more than 340 days—before the matter eventually came before the family courts. When it did, a thoroughly nervous but courageous Veronica gave her own testimony and I, with others, stood to support her innocence.

I was able to tell the court that I had tried to help Veronica in her Christian walk for three months before the raids, though it was only days after her release that I realised she had been implicated. (She tells her own moving story of this period in the final chapter of this book.)

My main role in the family court was as an expert witness for the defence on occult issues. I was able to explain that long-standing experience helping those struggling to be free from the occult had enabled me to assess realistically the truth or otherwise of such people. Certainly, Veronica had had her struggles, but the battle had been long won. I was also able to assure the court that even if Veronica had remained as a pagan Wiccan there was not the slightest evidence to suggest that, as such, she would have physically or sexually abused her children. In fact, the known facts of the Wiccan way pointed entirely in the opposite direction. The Wiccan beliefs and practices aimed at life enhancement (though I considered that there was a huge spiritual shortfall), and every Wiccan witch whom I had ever known in a long evangelistic ministry to those in the occult would have run a million miles before wilfully abusing a child. Such was my evidence.

At the end of the ten-day hearing, allegations of child abuse—ritual or otherwise—against Veronica were completely dismissed and the children were joyfully returned home. Even as I write, both mother and children struggle, sometimes in tears of frustration, to come to terms with the year they lost.

In the wake of Liverpool came the more infamous Rochdale and Orkney cases. There were also several other enquiries or cases attracting only minor media coverage, notably in Derbyshire, London, Lancashire and Scotland. To be sure, some of the children taken into care in these cases had been abused, including Rochdale and the Orkneys, but many affected families were innocent and their children were consequently returned home by red-faced officials. Various local authority enquiries were set up, though strangely not into whether ritual abuse had been involved. The enquiries were simply to examine whether or not the authorities had followed the correct child-care procedures. The veracity or otherwise of actual ritual abuse was to be addressed on a national level when the Department of Health agreed to fund an investigation by Professor La Fontaine, of the London School of Economics.[28]

The possible

This category is a minefield of legal traps, incredible claims, heart-rending decisions and sufficient quantities of suffering to bring tears to the hardest of men and women.

Here you meet, perhaps, the distraught mother proclaiming to an often deaf, disbelieving world that her children have been the victims of satanic ritual abuse, often at the hands of the father. The context in which the accusations are made is frequently that of custody hearings where the happiness and health of both children and parents are at stake.

Who is to be believed? That is the heart-rending question.

The only clear-cut case in this category known to me involved thirty-five-year-old Mary, whom I supported via long-distance telephone over the Pennines. Her husband had been imprisoned for sexually abusing the children, but it was only later that two of the three children, independently of each other, began to tell Mum what had happened to them (the third child was too young to talk). Incidentally, the truth is often only offered by ritually-abused children when they are in safety and security, and time has done its healing. Even then, it comes out piecemeal, and not in any logical sequence. Those who disbelieve children's testimony are often the ones who fail to understand this crucial fact of disclosure. It is also true that children only have to put a word wrong and their testimony is ruled unsafe by the powers that be. It is incredibly difficult for a six- or seven-year-old to be word perfect, especially in the midst of uniformed strangers or in a court of law.

Mary's children eventually began to talk about rituals and, much later, how they were initiated into satanism.

'Even now,' Mary told me, 'the kids go back into self-hypnosis and are lost to me. They were so scared of Hallowe'en, even though their dad had been taken away, that I took them to Spain for a late holiday.'

The appalling truth, when it eventually unfolded, so angered Mary that she went to confront her husband in prison. The usual quick search in the visitors' room failed to find the knife which she carried in her cluttered handbag, and Mary was able to stab her husband twice in the chest and stomach before the wardens intervened. Police at first charged her with attempted murder, but when more detailed interviews followed and the full horrific story emerged, they realised that Mary's intention was to 'hurt him as he hurt my kids'. The charge was subsequently reduced to grievous bodily harm. It finally came out that the husband's family, with whom Mary had had little previous contact, had a long tradition of satanism and there had been several suicides in the family. Before Mary's court appearance, she found the charge had been reduced even further to common assault.

The probable

Young Fiona was on the crowded top deck of a red London bus en route to school when she suddenly began to talk to her foster mum about a 'black church' and rituals.

Experienced foster mum Penny knew it was one of those important moments when you allow the talk to flow, and yet with other youngsters and parents crowding around perhaps there was a more appropriate place.

'Do you want me to go back home with you now and we can talk there?' asked Penny, knowing that children need to be encouraged to face the past if they are to have any hope of coping with the future.

But school won. It always would for Fiona whose seven-year experience of life had normally involved living with cockroaches, sleeping three or four to a bed in her family of twelve, and adults who did 'hurting things' to her. Now, there were new things to learn everyday. There were other things to eat besides chips. She could even eat more than once a day. She was also learning to smile in a world that wasn't as 'jumpy and scary' as she first thought. Most of all she now knew that little girls could talk to grown-ups, like teachers and 'new mums', without being hurt every time. She had even learned that she was allowed to make up her own mind about certain things. On the red double-decker school bus, home and talk could wait.

Tape recorders are part and parcel of fostering so that exact information can be passed on to the social workers, and a child is not forced to repeat things too many times. What follows is, in the raw state, what Fiona said later in the evening, and it was offered freely and without leading questions:

> My dad took me to church and people were wearing black clothes. The witches were making spells about me and they were touching me. They were trying to hurt me with a knife and they done it to some of my friends. They told me to jump off a big wall and I said no. They said they'd kill me otherwise. And my dad took me to Hallowe'en and they tied me and touched me, and some of them done it with their willies and some of them were doing it with their hands. There were mans, and there was a man who was taking pictures and they put it in a book. And some of them were ladies, and men was taking pictures. And there, and in a church, there were cobwebs on the floor and there was a star hanging up and it had a devil on it. And the devil...and there was a snake and the star was black and the devil had brown clothes on...and there was a wall with rude pictures.

Fiona later gave an official tape disclosure at Great Ormond Street Children's Hospital in London, in which she added other thoughts and incidents:

* Her memories 'made her sad and want to cry'.
* Adults 'wore long black and brown coats so that they looked like witches'.
* Spells 'were being made and things were said in low voices different to ordinary talking'. The spells were said and then she was hurt.
* Four adults 'made spells in the dark church' where the windows were covered.
* She had to drink 'some funny stuff with a sour taste' (her face screwed up as she remembered). It made her tummy feel 'yukky' and gave her a headache and made her dizzy.
* Men and women made a circle and she was outside it.
* They were not kind. She tried to stop them doing things to

her, but they tied her up by her hands and her legs and she screamed and cried and no one attempted to silence her.

* Other children (brothers, sisters and friends, it was revealed in court) were tied up, and she heard screaming and crying.
* The 'devil church' where all this happened was 'scary'. She said that Jesus made her smile and 'there is no devil in the nice church that I go to with Penny'.
* The adults called each other by unfamiliar names, but she always recognised her dad because she could see his eyes.
* She was told that they would 'kill her' if she told anybody what had happened.

As a result of Fiona's evidence and that of six other children (a total of nineteen children were actually involved), her father, grandfather, uncle and aunt were variously charged with rape, buggery, indecent assault and cruelty, allegedly committed between 1978 and 1989. Among the twenty-eight specimen charges was that of Fiona being stripped, tied to a chair and molested at the 'devil church'.

Knowing that the defence would accuse the children of cooking up the stories between them, a number of precautions were taken. First, the children were banned from seeing each other for the year it took to bring the case to court, even though this robbed them of friendship, the only comfort some of them had ever known. The second step was to provide corroborating evidence wherever possible.

Every charge was upheld, except for the one in the 'devil church'. The prosecution hoped that sufficient supporting evidence had been provided. There was Detective Inspector Carol Bristow, who testified that the church in question, St Mary's, Northholt, was known to be used for occult happenings by unwelcome visitors. There were also church leaders and members, including the vicar, who all agreed that 'unpleasant practices connected with witchcraft' had taken place at Hallowe'en in various parts of the church and grounds.

Trial judge Mr Justice Capstick made much in his summing up of the need for the children's stories to be fully corroborated before he sent out the jury. In their wisdom or otherwise, the jury felt that despite the high degree of probability, the corroboration on the 'devil church' was not sufficient to remove reasonable doubt. On the other charges of cruelty and sexual assault, the father was put behind bars for life, the uncle was jailed for twelve years, the grandfather for four years and the aunt for eighteen months.

Nottingham, Britain's biggest-ever child abuse enquiry, also qualifies for this 'probable' category, though the social workers involved, together with the foster mums and the children themselves, would wish to go further. In their minds, it is as certain as life itself. This is also true for one member of the abusing family.

'I had to tell the police or lose him,' Jenny told me, nodding in the direction of her boyfriend, the father of her young baby. 'He told me he wouldn't stay if I didn't go to the police and tell them what was happening at home.'

What was happening at home was that nine of Jenny's relations and one outsider had been regularly abusing twenty-three children in the extended family in strange occult rituals at the local cemetery and in hidden tunnels. Jenny said that this had been going on for as long as she could remember. She was twenty-one years old when we met.

At the time of this conversation, my wife and I were playing 'host' at my last church to several survivors—adults and children—of ritual abuse from various parts of the country. We had come together as part of television preparations for *The Cook Report* on satanic ritual abuse. During a day of interviews and a short healing service, I had tried to help Jenny come to terms with the guilt she felt for "telling on them". The adults, including most of her close family, went to jail for a total of 150 years, partly as a result of her testimony. Jenny had been so conditioned by her upbringing that she was still trying to understand why her boyfriend thought her family was so wrong, and why they should have been sent to prison.

When all the children later disclosed what had happened, everyone—especially the social workers—were mystified. It was to be many months before they realised what they were dealing with, and when they did, nobody would believe them.

'The Nottingham case sums up the state of the argument in Britain over the question of ritual abuse,' writes Andrew Boyd in Blasphemous Rumours,[29]

> with believers (foster parents and social workers) and sceptics (the police and the press) frozen in hostile deadlock. It failed, the police would say, for lack of empirical evidence, while social workers would blame the refusal of the police to believe the evidence before their eyes. One side believed and so found confirmation, the other side doubted and so overlooked the evidence that was there—so each would argue.

This is not the place to retry Nottingham all over again. Both Andrew Boyd and Tim Tate (*Children for the Devil*)[30] have already undertaken this task—and done it superbly. Suffice to say here that both concluded that the Nottingham case was ritual abuse. They noted that the evidence came independently to the social workers from each of the children in separate and unconnected foster homes. It was only when the social workers began to collate the details that they discovered an unmistakable pattern.

At a medical conference on ritual abuse in Harley Street, London, which I was invited to address[31], a fellow speaker, Nottingham social worker Chris Johnston, told me: 'We tried to deny it all at the beginning. It was too awful to think about.'

She added that the team did not really hear properly what the children were saying for several months. The words were coming through, but they found themselves unable to give them their true meaning. Eventually, she and other social workers faced two possibilities. Either the children—some only toddlers—had conspired with each other to tell the same story, and this without seeing each other for many months, or what they were saying happened actually did happen.

Mrs Justice Booth, who granted place of safety orders, certainly agreed that the rituals had been 'satanic' and so too did the three appeal court judges who acknowledged that the children had been 'subjected to sexual and satanic abuse'. These rulings, however, were not considered adequate by police.

Chief Constable Dan Crompton said that 'any attempt to consciously or subconsciously fit evidence to a belief system has grave dangers…standards of evidence gathering, investigation and presentation have to be maintained if we are not to revert to the ducking stool form of justice'.[32] He stressed that he could not act on uncorroborated evidence (dismissing available adult corroboration as unreliable), and pointed to the dangers of untrained foster parents contaminating children's evidence and the lack of any other evidence to prove the charges.

Andrew Boyd concluded his Nottingham report with a telling quote from Mary Midgley, adviser to the Nottingham abuse enquiry. It is worth repeating. 'The children told these stories repeatedly and forcibly. They poured them out…they named tunnels…to which they had been taken for rituals, and without consulting each other they separately led their carers to the caves.'[33]

The probabilities/possibilities of Nottingham were mirrored elsewhere abroad—in Oude Pekela, Holland, a village of 8,000; in dozens of cases in the States and also in Hamilton, Ontario.

In this last case—Canada's longest abuse enquiry—children were taken into care in 1985 telling of strange forms of abuse, and it took until March 1987 before the wardship proceedings were completed. Again, no police prosecutions for ritual abuse were brought, but the Unified Court of Hamilton-Wentworth in an historic judgement recognised ritual abuse judicially in Canada.

> "The detail and the horror of the allegations [of two young girls] belied the capability of a child to emotionally or mentally construct such events without an experimental base...the children had either experienced cult activities or had been subjected to simulated activities to believe that they had experienced them."[34]

There are two other probable British cases.

1. Satanic marriage contract

Worcester Crown Court heard that Reginald Harris had drawn up a satanic 'coven contract of marriage' with a fifteen-year-old girl when he was accused of having unlawful sexual intercourse with her and her younger sister.

The court also heard how he used satanic rituals to frighten the children into submission. On 8th August 1990, Harris was sentenced to two-and-a-half years in jail.

'You took the trust and affection of these girls to seduce and corrupt them,' Judge Roy Ward said.

The only reason this did not make the 'positive' category of ritual abuse was the judge's implication that though Harris had ritually abused the children, it was only done so in a framework of pretence. Judge Ward said: 'You [Harris] aggravated the matter by seeking to obtain dominance of their minds by the *pretence* of witchcraft or black magic to continue to gratify your desires.'

A similar case had a different outcome...

2. Genuine occult interest

The prosecution suggested that Shaun Wilding had used

satanism as a trick to induce four boys to submit to sexual abuse.

Prosecuting counsel Malcolm Morse told Stafford Crown Court in November 1986 that Wilding had constructed a 'black magic sort of shrine' and that the boys were forced to form a circle while Wilding 'chanted in a theatrical cape pretending to call up the devil'. Mr Morse added: 'He [Wilding] gave every appearance, enough to impress the boys, of going into a trance and speaking in strange voices…and by pretending to be able to summon up spirits from beyond the grave.'

The court was told that all the boys believed in Wilding's rituals and ceremonies and were convinced that his satanism was real. Defence counsel Christopher Hooton accepted all the prosecution points as he submitted a 'guilty' plea for his client, but challenged the implication that Wilding had only used satanism as a trick.

'The defendant,' explained Mr Hooton, 'has a genuine and long-standing interest in the supernatural and the occult.'

Views like Mr Hooton's were obviously not accepted by Professor La Fontaine during her investigations. She allowed that three of the eighty-four cases assessed did have material evidence of ritual abuse, but she concluded that the ritual elements were secondary to the main motive of abusing children.[35]

The positive

For the sake of honesty and fairness, I have made the criteria for admission to this final category tough. The charges need to be in line with the elements in the earlier definition of ritual abuse, and those so charged need to have been found guilty without a shadow of reasonable doubt.

The blunt truth is that no criminal case in the UK has ever fully met these criteria, *nor is likely that any case will ever do so!* This is not because ritual abuse is a myth. It is because ritual abuse is not a recognised crime, and nor is it likely to be. One South Wales police spokesman put it this way: 'We will never use ritual abuse as a term because, after all the publicity and press coverage, we find it unhelpful. The term "ritual abuse" clouds the case and is unhelpful to police investigations.'

This was stated as Wales' longest and most expensive child abuse case came to a conclusion at Swansea Crown Court in June 1994. In this case, the police were probably wise to avoid the term 'ritual abuse'. For though the evidence from ten children included descriptions of adults dressing up for orgies in cloaks, and animals being slaughtered in a cemetery, any satanic or ritual element was most certainly secondary to paedophilic practices.

However, I was given to understand that whatever had happened, the term 'ritual abuse' would have been avoided.

This has not been the case in America where the only 'positive' ritual abuse convictions have occurred. Some fifty adults in the USA had been tried for charges relating to ritual abuse by the end of the last decade. Half had been acquitted, but the other half had been found guilty and jailed. However, to be brutally honest, the half that were found guilty are still being contested at the time of writing, or at least heavily criticised by opponents of ritual abuse.

It sometimes seems that when it comes to ritual abuse, the term 'beyond reasonable doubt' is just not sufficient. It would seem that an uncontested, acceptable verdict will only be achieved when both judge and jury, together with defence and prosecution counsel, just happen to be on hand actually to see the abuse happening, note its ritual element, smell the incense, and hear the agonised screams of the children.

The following ugly cases help us to see why this is so.

1. A satanist and his daughter

A satanist repeatedly sexually abused his daughter in a bunga-low which had a temple dedicated to the devil. Behind the tem-ple door investigating officers found a black priest's robe, a pentacle on the floor, strange occult symbols on the walls and witchcraft books on display.

The sixty-year-old qualified engineer stood in the dock at Winchester Crown Court on 9th February 1989, and looked apparently unconcerned as the court heard how he had made his daughter pregnant five times.

Judge Martin Tucker said:

> ...by the strength of your evil personality, you gave her little or no choice. You already were the father of five children and you made your own daughter pregnant no less than five times. After two mis-carriages, a still-birth and a normal child, there was another child profoundly mentally and physically handicapped...When you no longer got sexual satisfaction from your daughter, you turned to her six-year-old little girl—your grand-daughter or daughter, whatever you call her. One can only feel totally nauseated by it all.

The satanist admitted his guilt and was jailed for twelve years.

However, this was not classed as ritual abuse. Why? Because ritual abuse was not mentioned, despite the fact that the court was told that the temple contained an altar on which there were phials of oil 'used in perverted sex during black magic ceremonies'.

Judicially, ritual abuse never occurred.

2. Fascination for devil worship

Another satanist showed his great-niece 'no compassion or mercy' in making her pregnant at the age of twelve, Liverpool Crown Court was told. He terrified her so much that after the baby was born, she told social workers at his instigation that she had been raped by a boy in the park. In reality, the great-uncle had raped her two or three times a week for two years. He instilled silence through fear, killing two of her pet gerbils and feeding one to his alsatian.

After the birth of his son/great nephew, the satanist insisted that the girl call him Damien (the name of the devil child antichrist in the film *The Omen*). The judge in the case knew from the evidence and listening to the man that his satanism had caused him to act in the way that he had.

Judge Denis Clark told the fifty-seven-year-old man: 'Your fascination with the occult or devil worship played a part in impelling you towards this evil behaviour. Society abhors sexual abuse of children and the sentence must reflect that abhorrence.'

The man, who cannot be named to protect the identity of his young victim, was found guilty after a week's trial and was jailed for twelve years on 2nd July 1992.

Again in this case, no ritual abuse was mentioned in court. There are three possible explanations why the ritual element was not introduced. First, it is possible though highly unlikely that there was no ritual element present in the cases, for both sex and ritual play important roles in most forms of satanism, as we shall see later. Secondly, it could have been ignorance on the part of those prosecuting—excusable in the 1989 case when the term was not in general use. Thirdly, it is possible that the prosecution failed to introduce the ritual element because the judges and juries had enough horror to cope with. This has happened in other cases.

Deputy Official Solicitor Jim Baker, whose office has kept a special record of ritual abuse cases which it dealt with in England and Wales over a two-year period, said that there were even more cases with overtones of the occult. Wardship courts, however, did not dwell on these aspects when there was already overwhelming evidence of non-ritual abuse.[36]

Maureen Davies, of Beacon Foundation, who deals with

many ritual abuse victims in Britain, told me that she knew of 'many cases where the prosecution do not want to risk the outcome of a case by introducing the difficult-to-believe ritual abuse element—not when they have enough evidence for a conviction on straight-forward abuse'.

The final two sad cases unfortunately seem to meet all the gruesome criteria needed for them to be classed as 'positive' ritual abuse cases. But they happened before the term was coined.

Black magic rituals

Twenty-year-old black magic follower Grigori Rasputin regarded himself as the devil's disciple. He also believed himself to be a modern equivalent of the mad Russian monk, hence his exotic name adopted by deed poll. This was explained to Leeds Crown Court in June 1988 when he was charged with luring schoolgirls into satanic sex rituals.

During one such incident at his lodgings, Rasputin—original name, Keith Beck—attacked a girl 'to drive out demons from her body', then carved crosses on her body with an ornamental occult dagger before having sex with her. Rasputin's former landlady, Amanda Plant, also told the court of another occasion when he seduced a thirteen-year-old girl during a devil-worshipping ceremony inside a church. He was about to have sex with her when the minister came in. Rasputin grabbed his clothes and ran off.

'He used to pick up girls from a local school,' said mother-of-two Mrs Plant.

He brought two of them to the house. I knew he was involved in witchcraft and that he was using his room as some kind of temple, but I didn't know what he was doing to the girls. He didn't seem interested in girls of his own age. In fact, the younger they were the better. I think he felt they were easier to influence. He was twisted and evil.

Her common-law husband, Mick Steele, said: 'He [Rasputin] kept talking to the six-year-old about the devil. I had to kick him out.'

It was revealed that Rasputin had also given 'magic mush''' to a thirteen-year-old boy, and exploded a home-made bomb in a transit van carrying three workmates. The vehicle was badly damaged, but the men had escaped unharmed.

Were the first offences ritual abuse? They certainly involved children; there was physical, sexual, emotional and psychological abuse; the context of symbols certainly had magical and supernatural connotations, even of devil-worship. Rasputin frightened and intimidated his victims without a doubt.

Yes, it was ritual abuse, but the term was virtually unheard of in Britain at the time. Rasputin was jailed for life for sexually assaulting a schoolgirl, planting a bomb in his council colleagues' van, and supplying 'magic mushrooms' to the schoolboy.

Four jailed

Nor was ritual abuse heard of when Malcolm and Susan Smith and Albert and Carole Hickman were jailed on 9th November 1982, for what was definitely ritual abuse.

They admitted before a Telford court that they had sexually and physically assaulted four children during the course of satanic rituals. The sex frequently happened on an altar dedicated to the devil, and the children were convinced that Smith actually was Lucifer.

The trial judge, Mr Justice Drake, said that the children were 'mesmerised' by Smith's rituals. Smith was jailed for fourteen years, his wife for two years, Albert Hickman for ten years and his wife for five years.

We do not have to rely solely on the courts to establish ritual abuse as a reality. There are other reputable sources and these have not been afraid to name the unnameable.

The Official Solicitor of England and Wales revealed that 1% of the 1,294 wardship cases in England and Wales handled by his department in a period of two years involved ritual abuse elements. Deputy Official Solicitor Mr Baker said that these figures emerged after his staff began to notice a new and shocking trend in child abuse cases.

Ritual abuse was also acknowledged in the autumn of 1990, when a survey revealed the horrifying scale of Britain's child sex-abuse networks. Police revealed that 1,812 youngsters were known to be victims of paedophile rings in the three years before the survey, and at least five of the gangs were accused of satanic rites.[37]

'This is the tip of a very big iceberg,' warned Superintendent Michael Hames, head of Scotland Yard's obscene publications squad. He said that society could 'forget the old dirty mac image. They [the perpetrators] are essentially from middle class backgrounds, single, lived with a sister or mother and are unable to sustain an adult relationship. Something like 85 per cent have suffered sexual abuse themselves.'[38]

As already stated, the NSPCC also acknowledged at one point that up to nine of its sixty-six area teams were dealing with cases involving ritual abuse.

That was their view in a press statement accompanying their annual report in March 1990, but by April 1994 they had had a change of mind. Following months of vilification of ritual abuse advocates, especially by the *Daily Mail* and *The Independent*, *Daily Mail* reporters Tracey Harrison and Peter Rose got the NSPCC to contradict themselves and support Professor La Fontaine's report against ritual abuse.

'This report is in line with our feeling. We have no evidence of satanic abuse,'" said an NSPCC spokesman.

A final comment on ritual abuse comes from Ray Wyre, Director of Gracewell Clinic which gives extended treatment

and counselling to perpetrators. He acted as specialist in paedophilia and consultant to the Nottingham case, and he said, 'I
have worked with people who have abused in a ritualistic way,
and in this case [Nottingham] there clearly was ritualistic
abuse.'

Where to from here?

These two chapters which have put satanism and the occult on
trial show that there are strong charges to answer. Our main the-
sis, however, has been to show one of the major ways in which
satanism and the occult have grabbed public attention—
through our judicial system. Not only this, it is my proposition
that satanism and the occult are crippling many lives, and society so far seems to be turning a blind eye to this tragic fact.

In our investigation, good questions to ask at this point would
seem to be: Why are satanism and the occult so prominent
now? In a world so advanced as to probe the universe and think
it old fashioned to stroll on the moon, how on earth have we
given room to the weird underworld of the occult? Why is modern, scientific, computerised, sophisticated, push-button, technological man retreating into black magic, and how come a
superstition more at home in the jungles and accompanied by
native drums, is now throbbing and alive in the plastic and con-
crete of the approaching twenty-first century?
    The answers are incredible. The facts more than suggest that
they are part of a revolution now well underway in our society,
the effects of which may well eclipse those of the industrial one
two centuries ago.

4
The Quiet Revolution

We live in a hemisphere whose own revolution has given birth to the most powerful force of the modern age—the search for the freedom and self-fulfilment of man.

John F. Kennedy (1961)

Liverpool mum Veronica still racks her brains to understand fully how she lost her way, found it, and then lost her kids for what seemed an eternity. A terrifying truth dawns as her story unfolds: it could have been me—or you! The phrase 'there but for the grace of God...' springs all too readily to mind.

Veronica is in her mid-thirties, a proper Scouser—as Liverpool as the Beatles, and as attractive and waif-like as was once top-of-the-sixties-pops Cilla Black. Veronica was a product of a wild, anything-goes decade, floating with psychedelic feelings and swaying in harmony to a with-it rock 'n' roll generation. The new beat was rapidly replacing the fading moral drum beat of the austere fifties as new musical ideas bubbled up from its caverns and clubs, and a group led by Gerry claimed to be Pacemakers on their 'Ferry 'cross the Mersey'. Liverpool grinned along with a young and cheeky Jimmy Tarbuck and chortled at a tattifilarious treacle miner from nearby Knotty

Ash, and, like Ken Dodd's Diddy Men, the little people from the 'pool were ready to take on and beat the whole world. And they did—with a soccer ball! If in a rare year the city did not echo to the roar of a triumphant 'Kop', then it was up-the-road Everton 'up f' cup'!

Scousers were born and bred to chant and sing and laugh in a decaying post-war city dominated by a pre-war industry run by dinosaurs. Veronica and a million others with lilting Liverpudlian twangs either laughed hard or cried bitterly, or just existed in the apathy in between. Some were buoyed up by fame on stage, pitch or disc, and inspired a big-hearted people to rise up and fight for new ground—only to end up broken on it.

And that echoed Veronica's fortunes as well. She too was determined to overcome. The Mersey of life might flow by leaving only its scum of poverty and unpaid bills, but only losers gave up, and Veronica never saw herself in that category. Her answer was to strike out for self-determination—and even more so when a friend offered what seemed to be the right weapons to gain control. The witchcraft of Veronica's Wiccan friend promised ways of influencing the universal mass of energy, whether it was the stars above or the hopeful ones sparkling in her own eyes. Everything that existed, so Wicca taught, was part of the one force, and worshipping that force in the form of the goddess—Diana, Hecate or whoever—could make a difference to life. Why, you could even guide the force through the jams of life with the turn of the tarot cards, just as you might steer a car in rush hour. What's more, there was an A to Z of a thousand and one other occult controls on offer from astral travel to the zodiac.

Veronica had no way of knowing it then, but she was to be yet one more conquest in a quiet, hidden revolution that was leaving in its wake an occult way of living and thinking for hundreds of thousands. The pace of this revolution has gathered momentum in recent years as its heralds have been heeded and its critics ignored.

This revolution beckons man away from the rational and towards the intuitive; from thinking things through, to feeling his way through—and emotions minus mind equals a growing anarchy.

The consequent breakdown of order is detected in many areas:

* Liberals spare the rod of discipline and hard work, believing man to be an angel who only needs better surroundings/education/money to realise his full potential.
* Churchmen forsake the known ways (Bible, tradition, reason) and opt for what feels right (some untested inner nudge or a sentimental kind of loving).
* The new placebo generation prescribes alternative therapies with little idea of why, or how, they work other than they make both patient and practitioner feel right.
* Moralists declare the death of absolutes, and counsel people to do what is right according to their own feelings.
* Mathematicians detect chaos in life's foundations and query the sums of the past.
* Physicists take quantum leaps into misbehaving quarks, and prophesy the disintegration of the old order.

As Veronica and her generation were blown hither and thither by fickle feelings, they were also fleeing from an age whose gods were drooping:

The god of more—the one worshipped by post-war parents who promised their kids more than the pre-war years had ever given them. It sounded good. More education = good jobs = more wages = good houses, two cars, the colour telly and, bingo!—*success*!

'Rubbish!' responded the rebellious sixties' kids who

decided that the creed of More was less than divine. They dropped out into happy hippy communes for a decade of protest.

And then an amazing thing happened.

Flower power fizzled out and kaftans and beads were swapped for pin-stripes and brollies, the owners of which then produced the most materialistic society the world had ever known! Only in recent years has the hollow echo of board-rooms, penthouse suites and senior common rooms turned yesterday's hypocritical hippies into repentant prodigals, eager to make amends and change society from within. Now, the doors of industry, commerce and education are opening to welcome the non-materialistic world of visualisation, Transcendental Meditation, stress-reducing mantras and other occult-like techniques.[40]

The god called expert. This once-mighty deity shrank to size when it failed the prayers of its white-coated worshippers in their test-tube temples. It created its Chernobyls, but fell asleep like the false gods of Baal when asked to dowse the consequences. This god of limits had no cure for AIDS, not even the common cold. This god of the gaffes produced thalidomide instead.

The god of churchianity. This was the most feeble deity in our trinity, moulded in Bluetac so that it could be changed at a theologian's notice. Theology has continued to be the art of fitting this church god into any gaps left by the other two gods. As a consequence, everybody assumed that the church god was irrelevant—and they were right.

What do a people, including Veronica, do when their gods fail, or simply turn into swear-words? What is to be done when emotions leave you adrift in high seas with no compass or map, and life is lived at the butt end of a spent second millennium, and a third on a poisoned planet seems doubtful? Is there an escape route from a society that imprisons you as a digit in its computer data banks? And how does one stop a rape when the victim is a planet and the perpetrators are faceless moronic millions—yourself included?

How bewitching then must have been the whispers of a New Age full of secret personal and planetary solutions, whether heard in the back alleys of our stained cities or the pathways of our scarred countryside! How beguiling the Wiccan hint that we can recover hidden human powers lost for centuries, or the satanic message that the 'real you' can survive into eternity as your own god, no matter what the rest of humanity does! How enticing the ever-widening shelves of the spiritual superstore where you can pick 'n' mix and create your very own plan of salvation! You can make your own god in your own image to suit your own personal physical and emotional needs.

Just how on earth did this view of the world come to us, and how did we come to take leave of our minds to follow mere emotions?

Birth of a revolution

Whispers about new ages, the occult, witchcraft and especially satanism came originally from those classed as madmen and eccentrics at the turn of the last century. People listened at first only for a laugh, for then the West had no need of a creed for the third millennium. Superman was born! Man, it was believed, had finally evolved and come of age to lift himself, by industry and enlightenment, towards new pinnacles. As a new century dawned on that romantic rose-tinted side of two bloody world wars and a dozen depressions, what need had scientifically sophisticated Western man of a new creed, especially one smuggled in from a cruel, poverty-stricken and backward East?

Our reintroduction to the occult—it having been forsaken during a thousand-year battle with Christianity and, finally, the

Enlightenment—was through Westerners returning from the East. They had fallen in love with the Orient, and consequently tried to smuggle in the ideas and beliefs that they had found there.

Before meeting some of them, look with me at the one idea that undergirds the occult revolution now being experienced in our culture. It can be summed up in one word: one-ism.[41]

One-ism

This is the first step into witchcraft, satanism and the occult. No gruesome hype of Hollywood surrounds it. No X-rated horror certificate accompanies it. It is guaranteed not to make you scream out in terror. Here it is:

> The universe is one,
> interconnected whole.

There! Not even a slight shudder, was there? And yet you could not be blamed if you had felt one. Those six words have caused all the agony highlighted in our previous chapters. They have kept millions in matchstick-leg poverty in the East for centuries, and they are responsible for more bloodshed, torture and deaths than all the battlefields of history put together. It would take a book to unravel fully the consequences of these six words, but here, in concise form, is the outcome of the creed of one-ism:

* There is no separate God. He, she or it is part of the force, just as is everybody and everything. (Opinion polls regularly show that 80-85% of our population believe in God, but the vast majority reckon that God is only a force and only a fraction think that God is a personal being.)
  This means...

* Good and evil are not real, simply two sides of the same thing—positive and negative charges of the force.
Therefore...

* There is no right and wrong. We're all players in the game of life with no external referee. It's Monopoly, soccer or boxing with no holds barred. Rules may be briefly agreed, such as 'let love rule', but only as long as it suits the majority, so history teaches us.
If there is no right and wrong, sin can be redefined.

* Sin is spelled 'separation'. If everything is one, then the greatest evil is to cause division. Duality cannot be tolerated. All divisions must be healed or merged so that all is one (even male/female, creator/created, human/non-human, yin/yang, etc). One-God religions, like Christianity, which positively promote the above differences, are definitely frowned upon. Better to merge and have a new religion embracing all the New Age.
The next step is to...

* Devalue life and death. If all is one then we are simply re-absorbed into the universal energy for recycling.

* Reincarnation helps us to improve our lot, or to make amends for previous lives. (Actually, this does not logically flow from one-ism. It's an idea tossed into the salad of Eastern thought to make it more palatable. Polls show that approaching a third of British youngsters now think they have more lives to come.)

* As a result of reincarnation Easterners think that helping people may damage your health—and theirs! The down-and-outs, the dregs, the sick and dying are meeting their karma; paying for the wrongs of past lives. To help them in this life is to hinder their progress to the next. Thank God for the Mother Teresas in the world of karma.
And if everything is one force, then...

* The force can be influenced, maybe even controlled, if all is

one and humans are part of it. Therefore a spell, curse, ritual or other hidden occult trick can affect another part of the energy (ie, another person—lover, boss, unpleasant neighbour, etc).

* Humans lose their status and become just blips of universal energy; no different from cockroaches, weeds or a dried frisbee of cow dung. Nature's terrorists therefore feel justified in fire-bombing humans to protect the rights of animals and trees.

    Perhaps the most remarkable outcome of one-ism is that...

* People, and even princes, can talk to the trees and plants! Why not, if we are all part of the same force?

Crazy? No, not really. Simply a logical outcome of the belief that the universe is one interconnected whole. Amazing what can come out of just six simple words, and how little it takes to start a quiet revolution in the mind of a nation.

Now, meet those who introduced the words and started our culture rolling away from the rational and towards the intuitive; away from our reasonable Christian heritage and towards the embrace of the East—and the occult.

Madame Blavatsky

'Christianity and the West must be made to respect their Indian betters,' proclaimed Madame Helena Petrovna Blavatsky, founder of the Theosophical Society in 1875 and the mother of modern Western occultism. The masters—wise men hidden around the world—came through to her, she claimed. Through automatic writing in trance state they gave her guidance, later published in book form as *Isis Unveiled* and *The Secret Documents*. The messages stressed that East was good and the West was decadent—especially Western science and Christianity.

At the same time that theosophists began to attract attention among the drawing-room aspidistras, another occult personality was in the making.

MacGregor Mathers

This dictatorial and flamboyant character, together with North-East London Queen's Coroner Dr Wynn Westcott and an elderly physician, Dr Woodman, founded in 1888 the first temple of the Hermetic Order of the Golden Dawn. They and their successors are credited with the preservation of all Western occult and esoteric traditions prior to this period, and the promotion of them into the present century.

Leading occultist Francis King wrote that the Golden Dawn 'members, although few in number, exerted an enormous, while sometimes hidden, influence on their own time and times since'.[42]

The order originated from German Rosicrucian and masonic documents, but it was Mathers who claimed its leadership after presenting rituals and magical workings from what he claimed were superhuman 'Secret Chiefs'—not unlike Blavatsky's 'Masters'. He wrote that 'the Knowledge' had been 'obtained by me from them in various ways, by clairvoyance...by astral projection on their part or mine...at times by Direct Voice audible to my external ears...'[43]

Among the members who gathered in the secret temple in the back streets of the capital were the Irish poet W.E. Yates and the Great Beast himself...

Aleister Crowley

If Blavatsky was the mother of modern occultism, Crowley was certainly the father—though the idea of them sharing the 'birth bed' together is an unlikely thought. For one thing Crowley was not born until the year Blavatsky opened her Theosophical Society, and for another, he didn't appear to care much for the Madame. He nicknamed her Jack the Ripper! Cordiality is not a strong virtue in the occult, and almost entirely absent from Crowley's character.

If there was one thing that Edward Alexander Crowley (Aleister, by later choice) learned well before graduating from Cambridge, it was that he wanted to be a magus—a master of the occult. Faced with the ever-increasing bank of human knowledge, he declared, 'I must find a material in which to work which is immune from the forces of change.'

His biographer, John Symonds, stated that Crowley found that 'only magic could guarantee immortality...he was attracted to its darker side, the so-called black magic, which was conducted with the assistance of Satan'.[44]

Crowley was born of devout Plymouth Brethren stock where it was never Christmas (too pagan) and there were no toys (too frivolous). The boy often went with his father preaching to convert the villagers of Warwickshire (and later Surrey) while thundering against Papists and Protestants alike. His mother he hated, he stressed in his first attempt at an autobiography, *A Boyhood in Hell*.[45] Despite this, Crowley in his junior years saw himself as a 'Christian knight doing deeds in holiness and valour'.[46] The first turning point in young Aleister's life came at the age of eleven when the father he respected died, and it coincided with his growing fascination for the Book of Revelation.

He fell in love with the False Prophet, the Beast whose number is 666, and the Scarlet Woman. He no longer wished to be a Christian Knight. The elders and the harps began to bore him, and one day he discovered that his sympathies were entirely on the side of the enemies of Heaven. What Crowley had once loved he now hated. He was unable to say why he had gone over to Satan's side; forty years or so later, when he wrote his autobiography, it still puzzled him, and he died without knowing the answer.[47]

Maybe it was because of his hated domineering mother, who often told him that he was 'behaving like the Great Beast', and he finally believed her. Maybe it was because there were never any reasons given for faith by his mother, 'a brainless bigot of the most narrow, illogical, inhuman type'.[48] Reading between the lines, a more charitable view might have been that poor Emily Bertha Crowley was a devout Christian soul with little education and little understanding of how to bring up a strong-willed child. God knows—and we shouldn't judge too harshly.

The budding Great Beast—he took that title to spite his mother—came to look on Jesus as weak and insipid, according to biographer Symonds. Crowley consequently began to see Christ as the false messiah, and opted to follow Satan who seemed to be stronger, and therefore an ally whose company should be cultivated.

But was it really all as simple as that? As we have noted, Crowley himself was unable to decide why he chose the satanic way. Does Symonds guess wrongly also when he blames an overstrict Christian upbringing for Crowley's reaction against Christianity? And then there is Israel Regardie who, as an occult student of Crowley's, detested his cruelty but later, when his master had gained his reputation, claimed that 'he possessed a magnificent difference which makes him altogether dissimilar to any other of the spiritual, metaphysical or philosophical instructors of our time'.[49]

Whether nature or nurture was the main force in moulding Crowley's character, we will probably never know. However, two episodes certainly give some hints.

'I caught a cat,' wrote Crowley looking back on his early years and the time he tested whether or not a cat really did have nine lives.

> …having administered a large dose of arsenic, I chloroformed it, hanged it above the gas jet, stabbed it, cut its throat, smashed its

skull, and, when it had been pretty thoroughly burnt, drowned it
and threw it out of the window that the fall might remove the ninth
life. The operation was successful. I was genuinely sorry for the
animal; I simply forced myself to carry out the experiment in the
interests of pure science.[50]

Crowley seemed to be at war with the conscience which he felt
had been stamped on his young life by Christianity. Once,
when he was worshipping before one of the greatest sights of
South India, the Hindu Temple of Shivalingam, it came to him
that Western man was 'blasted' by his conscience, saying that
Europeans 'cannot escape from their animal appetite, yet suffer
the tortures of fear and shame even while gratifying it...We
resort to suppression, and the germs create an abcess.'[51] It was
only after years of searing the conscience that he was able com-
fortably to boil down life to one commandment: *'Do what thou
wilt shall be the whole law.'*

In Christian terms, Crowley sounds like a fairly wilful, good
old-fashioned sinner who hates to have any god, or body, tell
him what to do. In biblical terms, he sounds just like the original sinners in the Garden of Eden.

The second notable incident occurred in Cambridge when, as
an undergraduate, Crowley had an ecstatic spiritual experience.
He describes it in flowery, picture language—this aspiring poet
rarely used plain English—in the preface to one of his privately-printed booklets.[52] He implies that he had a battle with
something terrible rising up inside him: 'I was in a death struggle with self: God and Satan fought for my soul those three
long hours. God conquered—now I have only one doubt left—
which of the twain was God.'

Crowley implies that the devil got the upper hand, and on
reading his subsequent beliefs, it would seem so. Defining the
god who won, he once said: 'When you have proved that God is
merely a name for the sex instinct, it appears to me not far to

the perception that the sex instinct is God.'[53]

And again: 'O my Father, O Satan, O Sun!'[54]

We need more words about Crowley than most for he is a formative force for most occultists, and nearly all satanists. Talking with modern satanists, I get the distinct feeling that they would want to walk in the shoes of the Great Beast, though it must be said that this would make Crowley turn over in his infernal grave, if that was a theological possibility. 'Do what *thou* wilt,' would have been his retort.

Crowley and his associates in the Golden Dawn were all high-ranking freemasons. In a book on the inner teachings of the Golden Dawn, R.G. Torrens implies that all masonry once had the dark occult secrets, but had 'become…an empty form'. The real secrets of masonry had been lost, he wrote, and could now only be found in other organisations faithful to the Ancient Mysteries.[55] Crowley actually wrote some of the rituals and rites for the Ancient and Accepted Rite of Freemasonry (a Scottish degree which originated from the continent).

Mason grand masters were also responsible for the founding and structure of what is today arguably the world's largest occult society, the Ordo Templi Orientis (Order of Eastern Templars—OTO).[56]

Aleister Crowley became head of the OTO in the 1920s, adopting the name 'Baphomet' (this is characterised by the goat's head usually seen in the horned pentacle, the sign of satanism and the blacker side of magic). He introduced the OTO to Tantric sex magic (part of Hindu yoga) and the rest of his teachings came from the mysteries of the Knights Templar, Rosicrucianism and freemasonry.[57] He claimed to be the Prophet of the Aeon after a trip to Egypt during which his holy guardian angel, Aiwass, told him he had been chosen to usher in a new age. He introduced the OTO to the Law of Thelema (Greek for 'the will'). In Thelema, there are no leaders, no guides and no priests to tell a person what is right and wrong—

only individual will. The thelemic magical[58] force was said to be given to initiate humanity into a new aeon of spiritual growth and freedom: the Aeon of Horus.

'Crowley was greater as a man than any prophet before him,' according to Gerald Suster, a present leading OTO Thelemite. Suster was speaking shortly after losing his job as a teacher because of bad publicity about himself and the OTO in the *News of the World*. Suster extolled Crowley as 'the greatest mountaineer of his age, a fine poet, a chess master, an explorer and a natural magician'.

This 'great man' was the one who revived barbaric orgies when he opened his Abbey of Thelema in Sicily in 1921, encouraging women and goats to copulate, and the ritual crucifying of frogs.

This 'great man' went on to explain that a young male child was the best possible sacrifice in what is regarded by occultists as his masterpiece, *Magic in Theory and Practice*. This is what he wrote in Chapter 12, entitled 'Of the Bloody Sacrifice'.

> ...it was the theory of the ancient Magicians, that any living being is a storehouse of energy varying in quantity according to size and health of the animal, and in quality according to its mental and moral character. At the death of this animal this energy is liberated suddenly.
>
> For the highest spiritual working one must accordingly choose that victim which contains the greatest and purest force. A male child of perfect innocence and high intelligence is the most satisfactory and suitable victim.'[59]

Occultists dismiss this as part of Crowley's black humour, and point to the footnote which states that 'Frater Perdurabo [Crowley's occult initiation name] made this particular sacrifice about 150 times every year between 1912 and 1928'. Surely sensible people cannot believe this, say occultists. Surely they must realise that Crowley is not serious.

There is nothing 'sure' about this. Sensible people might take Crowley with a pinch of salt, but not all people are 'sensible', like the occult criminals of Chapters 2 and 3 of this book. They are just the sort of people to take Crowley seriously. And maybe this was just what the 'great man' really wanted.

Some occultists are so desperate to exonerate Crowley from child sacrifice that they claim that the use of 'child' is nothing more than a synonym for the offspring of a young animal. However, they fail to answer how the animal offspring is to be tested for 'high intelligence'!

In our occult 'hall of fame' we next come to one of Crowley's greatest admirers.

Gerald Gardner

As for this man's character, it depends who is talking. Some see Gerald Brosseau Gardner as the much-respected 'Father of Witchcraft'. Others describe him as a meddling fool who should have kept quiet, allowing Wicca to remain hidden in the shadows.

'I personally believe that had Gerald Gardner not taken the brave step to publish books on the Craft,' declared Fran Skinner in her *Witchcraft for the Non-witch*, 'our knowledge of our history, religion and traditions, would be in a very sorry state, with many more of the old prejudices still rife.'[60]

Following the repeal of the Witchcraft Act in 1951, Gardner was the first to come out of the closet, opening a witchcraft and magic museum on the Isle of Man and publishing books on Wicca, notably *Witchcraft Today* and *Meaning of Witchcraft*.

Among those who oppose Gardner as the Father of Witchcraft is one group whose beliefs Gardner himself would endorse. These are the dwindling number of witches who believe that witchcraft has always existed in Britain and that

Gardner simply led a revival. Anthropologist and Egyptologist Margaret Murray insisted that twentieth century witches were the lingering remnants of the pagans of old, but her theory was shot down by critics who found huge time gaps when there was no mention at all of covens and witches. Murray died in the sixties at the age of 100 after confessing that she was herself a witch.

Gardner was one of her close followers and in *Witchcraft Today* he claimed to have found covens that had been operating for centuries. The truth, more likely, is that he had met with a few like-minded souls interested in nature religions, probably those who had branched out on their own from other areas of the occult.

What is certain is that Gardner had a way with the press, and the media loved him, especially his open-air, sky-clad (nude), power-raising circles of dancing and meditation. Before long, there was a queue waiting to strip off and be initiated, and he was more than happy to oblige.

Modern Wiccans and pagans have spent much time trying to distance themselves from any forms of black magic and satanism. One of their embarrassments, consequently, is Gardner's early links with Crowley. Gardner was certainly a member of the OTO, if only honorary, and he quoted—some say extensively—from Crowley's works when 'creating' his workings and rites for Wicca. Robin Skelton, author and witch, stated:

> Gardner's work influenced the Old Religion deeply. His rituals owed much to the occult and Kabbalistic tradition.[61] His admiration for the occultist Aleister Crowley led him to include some of Crowley's words in his rituals…the sexual rituals and practices of Hindu Tantrism crept into occultism in the nineteenth century and deeply influenced Aleister Crowley who, in turn, influenced Gerald Gardner and therefore Gardnerian witchcraft.[62]

Alex Sanders

This Wiccan witch claimed to be the King of the Witches, but only the tabloid press accepted him as such. Sanders seemed to blossom in limelight, and earned himself many Wiccan enemies as a result. Every time he hit the headlines, it seemed to be sex, money and power that were involved, and the more conservative witches felt threatened. However, he does have one real claim to fame as the founder of the second strand of Wicca, Alexandrian witchcraft.

There is a third strand, Dianic witchcraft, which owes much of its present popularity to feminism. This group look back to Margaret Murray for inspiration and consider that they are carrying on the Dianic traditions that Murray claimed to have discovered.

For a man, meeting Dianic witches can be somewhat disconcerting. During my few meetings, I have always detected a hostility which seemed to go beyond the fact that I was Christian. Rather it appeared to be my maleness which made me the enemy. Some were fierce radical lesbians, and talked mostly about worshipping the goddess, even to the exclusion of her normal male consort, the Horned God. To be fair, there are other Dianic Wiccans who are more liberal and accepting, especially if the man is willing to remain in the place they allocate for him.

In addition to the Gardnerian, Alexandrian and Dianic branches of witchcraft, there are those who simply term themselves pagans. Great overlapping takes place here and allows me to introduce Shan.

Shan

I could have chosen any one of a number of modern-day pagans to head this section, all having equal claim to do so. I choose

Shan for three reasons. First, she leads the House of the Goddess in London which attracts upwards of 2,000 to its pagan moon celebrations. Secondly, her work is a cross-fertilisation of many pagan traditions, and thirdly, she is the mother of Taliesin, who is potentially my 'God-child'! It is in this last personal area and Shan's attitude to it that helps us to understand the ecumenical approach of her paganism.

'Please make a small blessing for our son in the appropriate way of your faith,' Shan wrote to me shortly after the birth. 'My dad will teach him about Christ—he's a devout Christian. If Taliesin chooses that path we'll send for you to do the necessary.'

Shan and her house want the whole world to join hands and sing together, even if it is with different hymn tunes. At their pagan moon gatherings and Hallowe'en festivals can be found the whole range of pagans:

* the Celts—Welsh, Scots, Irish, Cornish. They can be seen in playful sword fights with...
* the Norse Viking warrior clans, who follow gods like Odin, and are full of Scandinavian legends. Then there are...
* the shamans of Red Indian heritage, or a thousand other races around the world. A shamanic witch-doctor is one who acts as a go-between for man and the spirit world, keeping one in touch with the other. Lastly, there is...
* the Mediterranean strain of witchcraft, taking in, among others, the ancient mysteries of the Greek and Egyptian legends.

Here, at Shan's place, you also find a scattering of magicians, especially practitioners of the new brand: chaos. This is 'punk' magic; angry magic. It is a reaction against all authority, tradition and leadership, and is not bound by any moral or ethical standards beyond those which the magician himself adopts.

Chaos magic is cannibalistic, feeding off any and every other path of the occult, and it is dangerous. It could be likened to playing Russian roulette. There are no safeguards, little control and total freedom to expand your consciousness, or blow it to kingdom come. Chaos magic boasts that it is the path of the 'spiritual warrior', the one who is prepared to risk everything for the sake of the prize. Greek mythology had its Argonauts gambling their lives to reach the Golden Fleece. Chaos magic has its 'psychonauts' willing to chance their sanity as they fling themselves into what they call 'the void' or 'the abyss'.[63]

The above presents a clear picture of how the various pagan paths interconnect. In reality, the true picture is more blurred. Certainly, these groupings in paganism do exist, but the pet hate of most occultists is to be labelled. They love to be thought of as free-ranging spirits. Individuals who describe themselves one way today may want to define themselves another way tomorrow. It all depends on their whims or feelings, for beliefs and practices are as permanent in paganism as fancy and fashion, though the pagan would prefer to describe changes as the outcome of his personal searching and evolution. This is especially true for those in the various branches of the New Age movement. More often, pagans will claim that they are into a mixture of traditions, some even to the extent of being involved in satanism. But that's another story, which we follow in our chapters on the shadow side of satanism.

These then are the alternative ways which beckoned people like Liverpool Veronica in the seventies, and even more so now. Back in the days when Veronica became involved, society could still afford to chuckle at witches with broomsticks. Now, many in modern society are acknowledging the presence of pagans and witches and even satanists. Radicals want to run out and join them, though they might get a fright if they did. Progressives and liberals cautiously welcome them for adding a splash of colour to the culture, while conservatives and traditionalists frown and mutter something about none of it being British!

What all of them seem to overlook, however, is that occult thinking is now present in the average thinking of society. True, not everybody is a raving satanist nor a member of one of the pagan activist groups we have noted. But some of their beliefs and activities are as normal as, say, cornflakes at breakfast time. The occult has infiltrated society and affected our view of the world and the revolution quietly turns on.

Come and see what I mean...

5
Revolution in the Arndale

Revolution n. forcible overthrow of government or social order, in favour of a new system; any fundamental change or reversal of conditions...

Pocket Oxford Dictionary

No jackbooted army struts the Arndales and high streets of Britain, but a revolution nevertheless quietly rolls through and along them. It is a bloodless coup, changing people's thinking at fundamental levels, and it is succeeding by obeying the first law of revolt: capture a nation's heart and then change the beat.

Stroll with me down the high street of Anytown, and notice the change in pulse.

The bookshop

The Bible is still the best seller, but occult horror writer Stephen King is, according to some, the world's best-selling author—after Barbara Cartland, that is. At least romance can still outsell the occult. Two decades ago, King introduced us to Carrie, the pimple-faced girl whose terrible gift cracked mirrors, made potato peelers fly and killed 400 of her neighbours.

81

Even today, readers find themselves sympathising with Carrie up to the last gruesome scream, perhaps wishing they too had the same psychic occult power to deal with the trials and problems of life. Before *Carrie*, there had been *Christine*, and afterwards *The Shining, It, Four Past Midnight*, and to date world sales of King's two dozen titles total well over 150 million. A dozen are box-office hit films and two of these have been transferred to the stage. When he is not writing as Stephen King, his nom de plume is Richard Bachman. Other occult writers, like James Herbert, also enjoy huge sales.

The Euromonitor Book Report for 1993 found that 'consumer interest in occult and horror books had increased, with more than twice as many people reading such books in 1992 as in 1981'.

Euromonitor also revealed that nearly half the population regularly read books—45% had bought two or three books in the month before the survey—showing that books continue to be a significant factor in forming public opinion, and thus affecting culture.

The religious/spiritual section of all bookshops is now dominated by the psychic, the paranormal, the occult or Eastern practices. Not surprising, since only 3.7% of all books in 1993 were classified religious, while a fifth were devoted to the esoteric, occult and horror. Book club advertisements in periodicals aimed at capturing new customers are almost obliged to carry occult titles.

Library books are being borrowed at a slightly lower rate than sales, but again King and Herbert are found in the top 10% of most-read authors. King is in the top dozen with annual loans of over a million. Browsing through the non-fiction sections of the paranormal, witchcraft, the occult and horror it is noticeable that the books are not only well date-stamped, but that new date sheets are pasted on top of old, often forming a stiff fly-leaf. The occult is obviously in demand.

Children's section

Enid Blyton competes with demons and monsters, and the children's adventures of yesteryear somehow pale when compared to instructions on how to perform a satanic black mass.

> Hundreds of black-cowled figures kneel at prayer in the dark-vaulted church...a golden chalice is being passed...blood drips from the vampire fangs. He hands you the chalice and you have to drink. It is human blood cursed in death's name. It curdles in your stomach, and you are seized with a palsy.[64]

The Evangelical Alliance purchased a selection of children's books to test the extent of the junior occult diet, and reported that they had 'found descriptions of vampires, werewolves, demons, haunted houses, ghosts and spectres...One book encouraged children to participate in fringe areas of the occult including testing their extra-sensory perception (ESP) and experimenting with pyramid power.'[65] Another book detailed 'certain times of the year when the evil powers walk abroad and when it is easiest to get in contact with them'. This was followed with a chant 'to call up the devil spirit'.

The EA and others suggested to society at large and children's publishers in particular that changes might be wise, considering the numbers of psychologists and social workers dealing with the impact of the occult diet.

In the two years following this balanced report, small improvements were noted. For instance, Teresa Tomlinson's *Summer Witches* became *The Secret Place* when Walker Books brought it out in paperback, though the story remained unchanged. This happened because pressure was applied by concerned parents to schools who, in turn, passed on anxieties to an educational book club who then required Walker Books to 'drop the witch' as a condition of placing a large order.[66]

Other parts of society, however, remain unmoved. Unconvinced is *The Independent on Sunday* journalist Rosie Water-house, who has earned a reputation for questioning the role of evangelical Christians, especially in relationship to the occult. She, together with co-writer Sarah Strickland, was dismissive and critical in an *Independent* article entitled 'Witch-hunt is launched over books and TV'.[67] The tone plainly supported those who believed that warnings about the occult and children amounted to unnecessary censorship. She quoted publisher after author talking about their concerns...

'I think it is terribly sad and rather absurd' (Walker Books spokeswoman).

'I believe that as writers we have got to resist this. It has almost reached the point where an unofficial censorship is in operation' (Helen Cresswell, author).

'We don't see anything wrong with that tradition [magic and witches] as long as it is responsibly handled' (Anna Home, head of Children's Programmes at the BBC. She was responding to criticisms that the serialised *Moonbeam* had irresponsibly taught 'young children about devil worship'.)

Some other parts of society actually consider it a duty to prime the next generation about the occult.

All pagans with media skills are being urged to 'remember the children, and get writing'! One example of this encouragement was 'All-in Vayne' staff columnist in *Pagan News* (Julian S. Vayne). His basic proposition was that children should be catered for at the same level as adult occultists.[68] Warming to his subject he explained: 'Thousands of books have been published on all aspects of the occult; indeed the demand for esoteric literature is such that even specialist works such as those on Enochian Magick and obscure mythologies are viable for publishers.'

Vayne is certainly right about this. Watkins Bookshop, which specialises in the occult, has approaching 15,000 titles on the shelves of its two-storey shop off Leicester Square, London.

Mr Vayne comes to his main point:

> Amidst all this, we tend to forget our duty to teach, train or at least interest the next generation in something more than just "conventional" life. It is this work which many writers of children's fiction are doing today. The fictional medium provides an opportunity for children to come into contact with occult concepts in such a way that they are not indoctrinated.

All-in-Vayne adds that there is literature already available which will inspire:

> The novels of Alan Garner, like those of Louise Lawrence, demonstrate obvious magickal elements to the trained eye, whilst on the surface being simply good fiction. In *The Owl Service*, Garner gives a modern re-telling of the Celtic Blodeuwedd legend; in *Red Shift* he explores the nature of time, and both books would be certain to fuel the flames of a budding adept. Children's novels that touch upon the occult are many, and most of them are exceptionally good.

All-in-Vayne adds that women seem more suited to write of magic, such as 'Penelope Farmer, Ursula Le Guin, Susan Cooper, Catherine Darby—the list seems endless'.

He also recommends many 'good non-fiction works' aimed at children. 'Pat Hodgson's *Witchcraft and Magic* is an excellent book, covering subjects from Alchemy to I Ching, and John Dee to the Mother Goddess, all in a lucid and balanced way.' All-in-Vayne saves his best praise for the well-known *Earthwitch*, by Louise Lawrence. Not only was it excellent for kids, he believed, but it also offered 'the seasoned occultist much, particularly in explaining the dynamic equilibrium between the dark and light faces of the Goddess'.

It is not only *Pagan News* that wants to prime children, so too do some teachers. Parliament noted this point when

Baroness Cox told the House of Lords that 'there was evidence that many schools were flouting the provisions of the 1944 Education Act relating to the teaching of RE...In a small number of cases RE was being used to introduce children to the occult.'[69]

The last words on children's books go to Richard Wilkins, general secretary of the Association of Christian Teachers (ACT). In a lead letter in the *Daily Telegraph*,[70] he wrote that ACT had received

> frequent complaints from parents about school books where witchcraft is perceived to be a major theme. These parents are most troubled when the books are part of a reading scheme. In such instances, it is difficult for them to ask for their children to be given alternatives without appearing to cause some disruption to the flow of learning...
>
> Today's parents are conscious of a steadily growing occult subculture; in particular, they are worried by the inroads this movement is making through officially-approved children's books. These concerns should not automatically be branded as 'paranoia', a condition which unfortunately does exist and the ravages of which we try to subdue. However, even if educationists from outside the Judaeo/Christian/Muslim traditions chose to describe as 'paranoid' all parental worries on this score, publishers would still be wise to understand their market.
>
> The chief business of reading specialists is not to confront adult psychoses, let alone religious convictions; it is simply to teach children to read.

The toyshop

Frankly, I'm embarrassed by some of the extreme Christian views on toys. This is one high-street stopover that I would choose to pass over, but that would not help our tour of the occult in society. Let me start with the positives.

Children need fantasy and wonderment; vehicles to transport imaginations to destinations of mystery and excitement, and yes, even, dare I say it, magic! Enchantment is part of childhood and adds to the images from which they then make sense of their environments and life itself. The sponge that is the child's mind soaks up every incident and image which, in these modern times, comes from television, parents and then toys and playmates. (Parental influence is probably secondary in the average home where children watch TV nearly as much as they study in class.[71])

Adapting some of the ideas of Swiss psychologist Jean Piaget and others[72], we could say that healthy toys should be fun, they should arouse curiosity ('What happens if I throw my porridge-filled Tonka truck in Daddy's face?'); they should encourage experiment ('Whee! See how fast I can go?'), inspire changes in behaviour and thinking ('Ouch! that was too fast!'), and help to revise old ideas ('Next time, I'll wear my knee-pads'). Healthy toys should reinforce positive values, especially those taught in the home. Now, all these good points can be stretched to extremes by the anti-golliwog faction, the anti-sexists and anti-war brigade—and all that's then left is Lego and a lump of clay! This being understood, and with commonsense as our guide, browse with me through Anytown Toyshop.

At the time of writing, the classic 'horror toys' are fading in popularity. *Dungeons and Dragons* with its curses, spells and death potions now only rates a double stand instead of wall-to-wall shelving. It still, however, exerts an occult influence over the sizeable seventeen to twenty-five-year-old market, and there is still a large question-mark over its adverse influence when Pat Pulling's research into D & D-related suicides are taken into consideration[73]. Also past their peak are positive-thinking, man-needs-no-God *He-man* and *Masters of the Universe*. Even the pure Zen Buddhism of *Star Wars*, Yoda and

Ewok toys have grown dim in the expensive glare of Nintendo and Sega.

Super Mario, *Mortal Kombat* and *Spiderman* are the technological blood-and-thunder inheritors of Game Boys. And what could be more harmless than the TV ads of a happy, smiling Super Mario jumping obstacles to grab the treasure? It's not until you pick up the super-glossy games magazines that you find that the occult is now being served with silicon chips. Every other action-packed page seems to feature the occult in one form or another.

At the top of the charts are *Super Ghouls and Ghosts*, *Magical Quest*, *King Arthur's World* and *Mortal Kombat*, in which 'the losers' souls become Shang Tsung's life-force and keep him young'. Fighting characters in *Mortal Kombat* include Raiden, the thunder god, plus a reincarnated spectre and an occult monk.

Some of the games were eventually grudgingly accepted as violent and unsuitable for young children, and Nintendo agreed to remove extremely gory bits, especially the death scenes from *Mortal Kombat*. The Japanese company later did a remarkable U-turn when in September 1993 it adopted a cinema-style ratings system, and thus tacitly accepted that some of its games were unsuitable for minors.

Then there are the 'god games', like *Powermonger* with the full range of occult and psychic powers, but 'you'll need to sacrifice alarmingly large chunks of your social life in order to cope with the shockingly steep learning curve', warns a reviewer. In another game you can 'call on the gods to bless you with their power' and cast magic spells, plus other normal practices of witchcraft and satanism.

Turning to the magazines' 'Agony Aunt' pages, the intensity of the young gamesters becomes evident. One boy asks for help with *Zelda III*, obviously having spent days, maybe weeks, trying to out-puzzle her ultimate magic before finally writing in.

Another correspondent asks for help with a similar game, adding, 'I'm starting to go insane!' He isn't, of course, but it does indicate the intensity of some players.

Page after page could be filled on the games' occult contents. But let's not get carried away and imagine millions of bewitched, demon possessed computer kids ready to set up satanic covens and become the next generation of criminals. Without overstating the case, it is reasonable to acknowledge that we are allowing our children on a daily basis to play in, and act out, a pagan occult world which leading psychologists and Christian leaders alike suggest is not the healthiest of environments.

Some points need noting especially:

1. These games are fun, arouse curiosity and encourage experiment, but they can also inspire a change in behaviour and thinking (according to our earlier synopsis of psychologists' ideas). This change, reinforced by other occult trends in society, will certainly not be in line with the positive Christian values in which our society is rooted, but according to the new wave of pagan thinking.

To say that we are breeding a generation of pagans may be going too far. But not by much.

There are no studies that I know of on the effects of belief systems on kids. But there are innumerable studies to prove that children are deeply affected by the latest games. Children who regularly play video games admit that they can be addictive and lead to them acting out the violent scenes that are an intrinsic part of many games. This was the finding of researchers from Aston University (October 1993). In their survey of 150 children, 60% had witnessed other children mimicking violent games, 80% lost their tempers when playing video games, and 58% of the children themselves said that they thought the videos made them more violent.

It was information like this that eventually forced Home Secretary, Michael Howard, to give in to the demands of a curb on video nasties by MP David Alton and others in April 1994. The final straw which broke the establishment's resistance was the public announcement by Professor Elizabeth Newson and other leading psychologists that violent videos really do affect children's behaviour.

2. Most games follow the best possible educational practice. We remember about 10% of what we hear, 20% of what we see, but up to 60% of what we see, hear and do. This is the pattern of fantasy and computer games, and when repeated daily, often for hours on end, they become the ingrained core of life.

3. It is true that teenage fantasy-gamers are less likely to lose contact with reality when they come from stable, loving, down-to-earth families. Healthy homes keep fantasy and reality apart from each other. However, one in three teenagers now comes from an unhealthy, unstable home broken by divorce. Escapism is the first rung on the ladder to creating a fantasy world. Those dealing with upheavals, rejections and resentments of broken homes and the other tragedies of life are vulnerable, and distinctions between fantasy and reality can blur too easily. Two instances come to mind:

In August 1987, thirty-two people were killed or injured in the Berkshire village of Hungerford by Michael Ryan after he received a challenge to 'kill his fellow Terrans' in an occult mail order fantasy game. At the time he received the instructions, Ryan was fifth in the game's league with the Swindon War and Fantasy Games Club, and he had to score more points by showing that he could kill the 'Terrans'.

'It was obvious who the Terrans were,' said Mr Paul Borreson who ran the club with his brother. He was at pains to stress that it was 'rubbish' to associate the instructions with Ryan and his killings. 'They [the Terrans] were his rivals in the game. There are a whole range of ways of killing, such as sword fights, duels or even casting spells.'

Mr Borreson said that they had 'rested' the games for about two weeks after the Hungerford killings. During this time they 'made them even more normal, even more game-like'. The company then resumed normal trading.

Thames Valley police confirmed to me that the fantasy games had been one of their lines of enquiry after the shootings. The official police report stated that Ryan 'was a man without friends who with his mother created a world of fantasy around which much of their lives revolved'.

Ryan was known as Phodius Tei in the postal game called *Further into Fantasy*. He played out the role of a high priest to a serpent god and was fearless and cruel. Ryan was sent the following instructions: 'When at last you awake, you are standing in a forest. There is a throbbing in your head, a madness... You know what to do, what power is to be gained by this.'

This was posted to Ryan just six weeks before his murder rampage which began with the killing of a mother in Savernake Forest. Another instruction to Phodius Tei reads: 'Rifle in hand ready to fire, you... begin to head down the stairs.'

In a shouted conversation from Ryan's top-floor refuge in the school in which he was eventually cornered, Ryan was asked by Police Sergeant Paul Brightwell if he knew how many he had shot.

'I don't know,' Ryan shouted back. 'It's a bad dream.' Minutes later he shot himself.

Another who found reality blurring into fantasy was sixteen-year-old Darren Fowler who modelled himself on Ryan when he blasted his way into his school with a shotgun, injuring the deputy head, a teacher and two young pupils.

The Oxford Crown Court judge on 24th June 1988, ordered that Fowler be detained for life after being told that the boy was out to kill his rival for the affections of a sixteen-year-old girl. The unstable loner embarked on his deadly mission not as a result of fantasy games, but after watching a violent occult video called *Critters*, in which a boy takes his father's gun. Darren armed himself with his father's shotgun, ammunition and two sheath knives and headed to Ferres School in Higham Ferrers, Northamptonshire, from where he had been expelled three months before.

This video-related story leads us naturally on to our next high street call...

The video shop +

The plus sign stands for the cinema as well as television. The following research can be checked by any reader with an evening to browse through his or her own town's largest video rental shop.

Occult and horror form one of the major categories for any video outlet. I popped into my local Ritz shop and counted nearly 150 occult titles in their own special section, including *The Evil Dead*, *The Curse*, *Amsterdamned* and *Friday the 13th*. The manager reported a thriving business in what he classed as a specialised market.

However, this specialised theme has increasingly been bleeding into the top-of-the-pops section, open to both children and adults. The occult is now a regular feature in popular dramas, comedies and thrillers. For instance, the highest-grossing film to be shown in Britain's 435 cinemas was *Ghost*, until the appearance of *Jurassic Park* in 1993. *Ghost* was also the most-watched film in the 1993 Christmas television season with 18.3 million tuning in.

Ghost is the romantic tale of a tragically-killed young husband contacting his wife through a psychic medium so that he can save her from a fate worse than death. *Ghost* is one of a further sixty popular family titles with occult backgrounds or themes. Others included *Chances Are* ('Alex has a lifetime of wonderful memories. Unfortunately, they are not his—reincarnation'); *Hello Again* ('her life hasn't been the same since her death'); *Flatliners* ('some lines shouldn't be crossed'), and *Second Sight* ('a tale of saucy sorcery in Salem').

On television, *Moon and Son* became regular viewing for 6 million on Saturday nights, and *So Haunt Me*, with its Jewish mother-in-law ghost, drew a bigger audience. *Steven Spielberg's Amazing Stories* demonstrated weekly how occult powers come to the rescue of many a deserving case. When it comes to the autumn season, every television channel seems to hit the occult overdrive button, until the advent of Christmas eventually inters Hallowe'en.

The occult's main penetration into society has been through the medium of comedy—a powerful force of culture change. Laughter allows the previously taboo to break through into our sitting rooms. Homosexuality could once go no further than public lavatories until society began to chuckle with the *Carry On* series and TV's outrageously camp *Are you Being Served?*. The occult has made similar inroads into society with dozens of humorous and seemingly harmless offerings like *Bewitched* on television and *Ghostbusters* on the big screen.

Children's television in the week of writing offers *Wail of the Banshee*, *Little Dracula* and *Ghost for the Day* for the tiny tots; *The Psychic Tea Room*, *Wizadora* and *The Real Ghostbusters*, plus others. Of course, none of these is going to create satanic monsters, and in previous times would give less cause for concern.

But consider this. Tiny tots and youngsters take in the occult, casting spells and calling up evil spirits as part of everyday viewing. It would seem reasonable to assume that, at the very least, a few would not depart from the way they had been shown.

Also consider this. Should we entrust our children for four or five hours a day to a total stranger, especially if we know that that stranger is feeding them a diet of witchcraft and the occult, often interspersed with violence?

Give the television a child until he is seven and it has him for life!

The music/tape shop

Records, CDs, tapes and tee-shirts are shot through with the occult. It started as far back as the Beatles who included the bald head of Aleister Crowley on their sixties album *Sergeant Pepper and His Lonely Hearts Club*. Through the seventies and into the eighties, those like Ozzie Osbourne even began to extol the virtues of Crowley's satanic thinking.

Now in the nineties, the occult is a fixture, and we would need a book to list its A-to-Z involvement in the pop industry. Space allows us to go no further than the first letter of the alphabet, but that is sufficient to help our understanding.

Abaddon, lead singer with the black heavy metal band Venom, said: 'I'm not ashamed of being a Satanist.'[74] He was speaking after a double teenage suicide had been associated with hidden occult messages.

Newcastle-born Abaddon claimed: 'It takes more than a subliminal message on a track to make a kid kill himself. We've been doing it for years.'

The messages played backwards included, 'I'll steal your soul,' 'You'll burn in hell,' and, 'Bleed for me.' These are actually no more unpleasant than the true words played forwards on albums such as *Welcome to Hell*, *Possessed* and *Buried Alive*.

Abaddon—originally the name of the demon who is the angel of the bottomless pit (Revelation 9:11)—said: 'I don't know whether the kids who come to watch the band know I'm a satanist, but I don't keep it a secret. I am a practising one when I get the chance, but we're on the road so much I don't really get much opportunity.'

The double suicide involved Raymond Belknap and James

Vance who were said to have shot themselves after hearing the words 'do it' on the record *Stained Class* by British band Judas Priest, a US court heard in July 1990.

Abaddon, whose real name is Tony Bray, added: 'All the top heavy metal bands use backwards tracking on their songs. It's a way of having a bit of fun with a record.'

Going on to others in the 'A' section:

The Accused snarl, 'I'll be glad when you're dead,' and sing about devil women and rape. They claim to be 'more fun than an open-casket funeral'.

AC/DC tell their fans: 'If you want blood, hell ain't a bad place to be.' They encourage listeners to 'rock 'n' roll to hell' and extol the virtues of the colour black.

Alien Sex Fiend are delighted to announce in their *R.I.P* album that they're 'feeling zombiefied' and are "dead and re-buried".

Antiseen boast: 'My God can beat up your God,' and then instruct their fans at full-decibel range about evil rock 'n' roll, hate and power and self-destruction.

Atomic Rooster assure their congregation that 'the devil hits back'.

Each one has many more titles but normal sensitivities about pornography prevent us adding to the list in this book.

The newsagents

On most town-centre shelves is a generous selection of occult literature, including the glossy *Prediction* and *Horoscope* and a variety of annual almanacs foretelling where turmoil will boil and which royals will divorce. You can also order one of three dozen further occult magazines and periodicals.

Most carry contact advertisements, and the reader—even the vulnerable, searching youth—is only a postage stamp away from life in a coven or satanic temple: One ad. claims, '20,000 lines *In stock* on Psychism/Mind Power/Healing/Astral Travel/Spells, etc'; another celebrates its golden jubilee year with a spell book *Discover REAL Magic*. The British Occult Church promises members 'Hidden Magic of the Cosmos". Residential courses are offered by others for beginners. In addition to all this there is the sixty-four-page occult *Consultants' and Psychics' Directory* offering past-life recall, individual elemental spells for your love life, parent-child horoscopes and tarot card readings for your future destiny.

The occult penetrates significantly into everyday life through the national newspapers. In my research into the occult I have collected two dozen thick A4 files, and a third of those represent press cuttings. One supporter of the Christian Response to the Occult was more scientific and disciplined when he analysed occult coverage in the press over a three-year period up to 1991. He took cuttings from the quality press and the front pages of the tabloids. The analysis is therefore rather conservative, and takes no account for instance of the popular fascination with astrology, nor stories where the occult is mentioned as a side issue. In pure hard news terms, he counted nearly 560 occult stories, almost one for every working day of the week. Press cuttings on satanic/occult crime generated three times as many press cuttings as did general stories on paganism and the occult or the New Age. Add to this the British romance with astrology and the psychic and you have what amounts to a daily drip-feed of the occult into our culture.

In addition to the above, all local papers carry advertisements for mediums and seances, astrology readings, hypnosis/yoga/alternative healing clinics and so on.

Computer centres

My research for this book led me to become one of the more recent citizens of a new nation which is set to take over the globe (according to *The Daily Telegraph*, 4th May 1994). The population of this nation is almost the size of Britain and is growing rapidly.

It is made up of 40 million people in fifty-six countries who are now connected to each other via the largest communications network ever built.

At the press of a button, I have a direct line into the very heart of satanism, witchcraft, paganism, the New Age and other branches of the occult. I can receive their literature, access their libraries. Read up on their latest rituals, talk to any who have modems, leave messages and receive them. Some of them even claim to cast their spells down the line.

The occult is in the forefront of the computer revolution in an electronic community where there are no laws, no controls and no censorship.

The prison

Your high street might not have a jail at the end of it, but many of the major towns do around my neck of the woods, and paganism and the occult have succeeded in gaining access.

As I write, it is announced that Prison Service Chaplaincy will be publishing a pagan section in the chaplain's working handbook, the *Directory and Guide on Religious Practice*. The areas of paganism being considered for chaplaincy coverage in jails are Wicca, druidism, shamanism and the New Age.

Of course, a mature democratic society feels it has no alternative but to let in what it sees as 'other faiths' However, society might do well to remind itself that freedom of belief is often set aside when one person's beliefs rob others of their freedom.

For instance, society restricts paedophiles in their beliefs about children and sex.

My research shows that paganism's occultic practices are causing many to lose their freedom. As we have already seen, many are actually in jail partly through their involvement in the occult. It hardly seems wise to provide prisoners with more of what put them in jail in the first place.

Restriction of others' freedom is among the root beliefs of paganism and the occult. They stress manipulation and control of environments and people. Wiccans cast their spells, blessings and curses, and thereby claim to have a strong influence over others, in fact boasting about curtailing the freedom of others.

Finally, the introduction of pagans into prisons will drastically restrict the freedom of all present prison chaplains. The chaplains will be forced to facilitate pagan rituals which are directly contrary to their beliefs. It could mean that Christian chaplains of integrity will either have to renounce the core beliefs of Christianity or quit the prison service.

Sundry calls

Local hotel lounges are regularly taken over for psychic fairs, often attracting several hundred over a weekend.

Then there are the local fairs with an assortment of fortune-telling tents and stands. Many of these fairs or fêtes are run by churches, who ironically often turn out to be the soft occult's biggest supporter. Our local high street boasted a fortune-telling tent one Sunday, and housewives queued throughout the day until 11pm waiting to cross an amateur lady's palm with £1—for charity, of course.

Odd, isn't it, how society raises money for its vulnerable members by using the very thing which is causing them so much damage!

The occult, mystic, alternative spirituality centre or shop is becoming a normal feature in most towns. Their numbers are now on par with those of Christian bookshops. The 62-page annual *Occult Directory* lists 654 resources in the high streets and towns of our land, which means that you cannot go far without meeting some expression of the occult. There are also approaching 300 occult and New Age periodicals to meet their growing numbers of occult followers.

Warning note:

Beware the vanishing occult shop trick which has become a regular feature of the last decade. The name to listen out for is Mr Daniel Hussey, of London. He has a habit of contacting local newspapers to discover the cost of advertising a new occult shop. He knows that advertising managers are always on the lookout for good news stories to pass on to the news editor. The next step involves a journalist telephoning local clergy and church leaders for comment and—bingo! An immediate front-page lead. Often churches have gone to the trouble of organising protest marches while Mr Hussey quietly does a vanishing trick, never to be heard of again in that area.

He tried it in my home town three weeks after I had been speaking against his plans to open up a shop in Teddington, Middlesex. I had travelled down at the invitation of MP Toby Jessel and the local action group to address a public meeting of 300 citizens concerned about Mr Hussey's plans. This particular occult shop scheme seemed genuine, and possibly was, for Mr Hussey had opened up a shop called Mystic Science in September 1991 in London, on Westminster Bridge Road.

When I was approached by journalists over Mr Hussey's plans for an occult shop near my home only a few days after returning, it seemed somewhat of a coincidence. I told the press that they were probably the victims of a hoax, and not to hold out too much hope of receiving advertising revenue from Mr Hussey.

Between 1st October and the end of November 1991, Mr Hussey and his 'black magic shop coming to town' were headline news in Woking, Sunderland, Bolton, Edinburgh, East Grinstead, Richmond, Twickenham, Aberystwyth, Dartmouth, Luton, Glasgow, Hereford, Grimsby and Grantham. On other occasions, he claimed he was moving into Bracknell and Blackwood, Gwent. And these are only the places my limited resources have managed to unearth.

Mr Hussey is, of course, doing nothing illegal. He has an off-beat sense of humour, or something! Even when I spoke to him personally after my own home town alert, he said, 'Of course I'm serious. I wouldn't be doing it otherwise, would I?'

All I can say in reply is, hold fire if a local journalist wants your opinion on the new occult shop opening in your town. Do a bit of digging.

Our final high street stop is...

The local

And where better to discover what people think and talk about, especially after tongues have been well and truly oiled? A vicar in the local towards closing time is often witness to a kind of spiritual olympics. Assorted owners of loose tongues often seem to be out to impress the 'padre' with astonishing spiritual feats involving energetic poltergeists, incredible premonitions, hauntings, and the reason why 'you don't have to go to church to be a Christian'!

Beneath the gruff exterior of the average bar supporter, there lurks a little spiritual boy trying to make sense of those experiences which contradict what happens at work. His wife, nattering in the lounge, needs far less alcohol to relate her spiritual experiences, which are broadly the same as hubby's.

It is amazing what people admit to believing when they drop their guard and open up to their friendly local vicar. It is in line with what national opinion polls have revealed.

Only 2% of readers of our most respected newspaper, *The Times*, said they definitely did not believe in the psychic and supernatural, and 64% said that they definitely accepted psychic phenomena, such as contacting the dead, poltergeists, reincarnation, hauntings, dowsing, premonitions and out-of-body experiences. The remaining 17% believed that the psychic 'probably existed'.[75]

A more recent poll conducted by Southampton University revealed that nine out of every ten people in the United Kingdom believed in the reality of at least one psychic occult phenomenon.[76]

This one fact alone—apart from the rest of this chapter— indicates that a people who once trod the way of reason are now more inclined to float through life on feelings. Our twentieth-century society is increasingly swinging back to paganism and superstition, because the gods fashioned by the mind have proved to have no power and little promise.

When 90% of our population accept the occult in one form or another, does it not strongly suggest that the nation's heart has certainly been captured and its beat well and truly changed?

The quiet revolution is on quite a roll. And it is not so quiet.

6

The Sliding Scale

My magical experience and studies have focused on Enochian...Crowley, and the Golden Dawn...At this time my work is towards establishing stronger links with Set [neo-satanists]. Before joining the temple I was using the form of Baphomet as my satanic image, and experiences with the Goat of Mendes led me to the Setian Path.[77]

The occultists of the high street fish with a variety of bait, and the potential customers—you and I—are invited to nibble as we float by.

But what then? What happens when the attractive bait does its job and a budding occultist is landed? I want to suggest that the buyer of the heavy metal CD or the pack of tarot cards in W.H. Smiths, or the occult fantasy game in the children's toy department can move all too easily from the point of sale to the covens of witchcraft and satanism. Those who begin to observe occultists in their beliefs and rituals soon notice a definite progression from one form to another.

This has been hotly disputed by those in the occult when we have debated it on television, radio or in print. Witches, for instance, vehemently maintain that they have nothing whatsoever to do with satanists, while satanists themselves will disown witches for merely "playing at the occult". Psychics, spiritualists and those in the paranormal will look down their pseudo-religious noses at witches and satanists, and those in the New Age will giggle if you suggest that they and black magicians are even on the same planet. Yet this progression is illustrated time and again in people's lives.

Take, for example, William Roache, *Coronation Street*'s Ken Barlow for the last twenty-three years. I am not for a moment suggesting that he is a closet satanist, but his ramble through occult spirituality provides an easy-to-see example of the progression to which I am referring.

Mr Roache—far more spiritually aware than his TV character, Ken—was at one time a keen student of astrology. At another time, in the late seventies, his spiritual journey took him to Stonehenge, where he appeared as a Druid, complete with flowing white robes.

'Studying with the Druids was only a step on the path of my quest for greater knowledge,' Mr Roache stated in his autobiography, *Ken & Me*.[78] 'I studied in many other areas and gradually came to certain realisations and understandings.'

In an interview with *Sunday Telegraph* writer Frances Welch,[79] Mr Roache said, 'Listen, I only want you to say this much about the Druids'—he held up a finger and thumb three centimetres apart. 'They were just part of my search and I've moved on.'

And that is precisely the point. The spirituality of the occult never settles in one place, for its number one principle involves a search for knowledge and inner satisfaction. Once the search ceases, so too does occultism. Occultism simply means 'hidden'. Occultism therefore necessitates searching to find that which is hidden. The occultist progresses from one piece of knowledge to the next.

Mr Roache, who still considers himself part of the Church of

England, despite his sojourns into other faiths such as Buddhism and Hinduism as well as the occult, believes firmly in progressive incarnations ('not reincarnation—that starts people talking about coming back as dogs'). The occult search progresses even beyond the here and now and into eternity.

Chris Bray's company, the Sorcerer's Apprentice, depends on this progressive search. Certainly, he would want to spell out the differences between the various paths of the occult, but he—like every other occultist—would be astonished if everybody was expected to serve a lifetime in only one occult discipline. The life stories of Aleister Crowley, MacGregor Mathers, Gerald Gardner, Madame Blavatsky have been nothing if not about progression from one occult form to another.

Progression is built into the testimony of those at what might be said to be the end of the occult line: satanism. During my research for this book, I was given a copy of *The Crystal Tablet Set*, a large tome handed to the initiates of the Temple of Set, a satanic group we shall investigate later. It included members' names and personal information and details of their spiritual paths. None started as satanists. All progressed there, and to avoid an invasion of privacy, I use their first names only. This is what they state about their own searches...

Frank: 'Years of study of mythology, both pagan and Christian, and the religions of the world, led me to the Church of Satan, and eventually to the Temple of Set.'

Gregory: 'My magical experience and studies have focused on Enochian, the Cthulhu Mythos, Crowley, and the Golden Dawn...At this time my work is towards establishing stronger links with Set. Before joining the temple I was using the form of Baphomet as my satanic image, and experiences with the Goat of Mendes led me to the Setian Path.'

David: 'My occult studies, over the last 15 years, have spanned the historical spectrum, from ancient Egypt and the classical mythologies to the music and literature of the pre-

Roman Celts, the ancient Britons and the Druids. I have also studied the cultures and beliefs contained in the Viking sagas, Runic lore and Woden magic.'

Jennifer speaks of coming through several spheres of the occult, including 'tarot readings...and the thoughts and teachings of Aleister Crowley'. She adds: 'I am at present obtaining different oils, incense and herbs...to make my own incenses corresponding to astrological signs, planets, etc.'

The list of personal searches goes on and on.

Like it or not—and many in various branches of the esoteric will not—the occult stretches along a line from Astrology to Zen Buddhism and people freely travel along it in both directions. Tarot card readers can no more divorce themselves from satanists just as witches cannot separate themselves from the Druids. Certainly they have differences but, like it or not, they belong to the one continuum of the occult.

In Christianity, there is such a thing as the Engel's Scale which is used to chart people's progress towards, and into, the faith. With apologies to its designer, James F. Engels, I have adapted it to illustrate how people enter the occult and progress through it.

The Occult Progression

Role of the occult	Stages reached		Curiosity factor
	First supernatural experience	-10	"Good grief! How did that happen?"
	Making sense of it	-9	"What's it all about?"
Presence in society	Dabbling	-8	"Can I make it happen again?"
Proclamation in the media	Study & growing knowledge	-7	"Why does it happen?"
	Grasp of the basics	-6	"So that's what it's all about!"
	Accepting attitude	-5	"It's not really OTT, is it?"
Personal persuasion	Invitation	-4	"Fancy a seance?"
	Personal need	-3	"Somebody, help me!"
	Challenge and decision to act	-2	"Should I? Shouldn't I?"
	Acceptance	-1	"Yes, I will!"

COMMITMENT IS MADE—A NEW OCCULTIST IS BORN

	Stages reached		Curiosity factor
	Initiation	+1	"I want to belong".
	Re-evaluation	+2	"What on earth have I done?"
	Growth in understanding	+3	"Where do I go from here?"
	Discovery of powers/gifts	+4	"Can I see into the future?"
	Adept or master	+5	"Now I've arrived!"
	More knowledge (boredom)	+6	"Oh no, I haven't!"
	New initiation	+7	"Here we go again!"

For clarity's sake, here is a brief commentary on the scale.

-10: First supernatural experience

'Good grief! How did that happen?' It could have been a pre-monition, an answered prayer, a ghostly apparition, a spiritually uplifting feeling, a ouija board session, a seance, even a 'meeting' with God—anything that awakens the spiritual.

-9: Making sense of it

'What's it all about?' We have always been free to set aside these incidences as fanciful products of our overworked imaginations. However, society's romancing of the occult means that we now entertain them and accept them, much more readily than in the past.

-8: Dabbling

'Can I make it happen again?' Men and women have a curiosity which stretches back to the Garden of Eden, and they begin to experiment.

-7: Studying and growing knowledge

'Why does it happen? Are there any strings attached?' At this stage there is an eagerness to learn; perhaps buy another occult magazine from the local newsagents, go and see those who seem to know (perhaps friends), or answer a local newspaper ad, or visit an occult shop.

-6: Grasp of the basics

'So that's what it's all about!' A growing awareness of the implications of becoming a witch, a tarot reader, a psychic medium, or whatever.

-5: Accepting attitude

'It's not really so over the top, is it? In fact, it's beginning to make sense.' Once a person accepts, for example, that the universe is one interconnected whole, and that one part of the universe (a human being) can affect another part (another human being or a situation, etc) then the occult is actually quite a logical path.

-4: Invitation

'We're meeting in the George and Dragon tonight, if you fancy a drink.' It can come from a work colleague or friend or relative. Most in the occult say they never 'evangelise' or try to persuade people to join them. They do. They wouldn't be human if they didn't.

-3: Personal need

'Somebody, help me!' An enormous culture barrier keeps the still mainly materialistic world away from the spiritual, but it is often no competition for the demolition forces which accompany personal need. Sickness, insecurity about the future, trouble in the love nest, loss of a loved one—any one of these can create unbearable pain. The slightest hint that perhaps a psychic show, or a seance, or an astrologer, or friends in a coven might be able to help is all that is required at this stage.

-2: Challenge and decision to act

'Should I? Shouldn't I?

-1: Acceptance

'Yes, I will!'

Commitment is made—a new occultists is born

+1: Initiation

'I want to belong'. This can mean a subscription form, taking certain oaths, or some form of ritual. Some of these can be quite bloody or pornographic in content.

+2: Re-evaluation

'What on earth have I done?' Newcomers to the occult begin to wonder whether they have made a mistake once a personal need has diminished and they get back into the normal world. Commitment begins to be questioned. Fellow occultists will be available for reinforcement.

NOTE: At this and other stages, occultists decide they want to get out, and they approach people like myself. There can be a great deal of fear involved when people feel out of their depth, especially when they have tried to control something which eventually begins to control them. This, of course, can happen at any stage from -10 onwards.

+3: Growth in understanding

'Where do I go from here?' The occult has a million and one paths ready to explore. To become a master or adept in one field of the occult can often take the equivalent of a four-year university degree course.

+4: Discovery of powers/gifts:

These can range from reading people's fortunes, casting spells and getting in touch with dead spirits. There are, for example, sixty-two occult techniques for divining the future, which range from using spent tea-leaves to dead bodies.

+5: Adept or Master

Many forms of the occult have a system of promotions and grades. You can get to the top, or just get bored. What then?

+6: More knowledge

It is almost as though knowledge or enlightenment becomes god, the driving force. It is noticeable that people often flit between branches of the occult in search of greater knowledge.

+7: New initiation

Often, the only way of getting new knowledge is to try another branch of the occult. Then comes a new initiation and the whole process begins again, and again, and again...

Three important points need to be noted:

1. People are individuals and this is only a list of steps that all will take on their way into, and their progress through, the occult. Not everybody will take these steps in this order. I can, for instance, think of quite a few for whom the very first step was "personal need". They cried out for help, and when no one heard in their existing environment, they began to look elsewhere.

It is heartbreaking to realise that every occultist I have ever met is a refugee from some form of dead churchianity. When they yelled for help nobody heard. It is even sadder to realise that these refugees think they have been in touch with real Christianity, when in fact they have been inoculated against the real thing by a dead form of it—churchianity.

2. Not all the steps will take equal time. There may be long periods between each, or several steps may be taken in quick succession.

3. The left-hand column of our scale marks out the involve 'conversion and growth'.

The occult's presence in society is there almost from the beginning, in the high streets of our communities.

The occult's proclamation of its beliefs begins at the -7 point when a man, woman or teenager decides to learn more.

The occult's persuasion comes into play at the invitation stage.

This scale for an increasing number heads in one direction—satanism and the blacker side of magic. And that's the next step in this book's progression.

7
The Satan Story

They lost faith in the Catholic church; they wanted wealth, fame and glory, none of which seemed to come from serving pilgrims. A number of members decided that the answer was to look to the opposition. If worshipping God failed to help them reach their desires, perhaps Satan would be more responsive. Their cere- monies would be on the same date as those of the Catholic church, but they would reverse all the rituals…An investigation in 1307 revealed that members engaged in strange rituals, some of which eventually became the basis for voodoo and satanic worship…The Knights Templar did not believe that Christ was the Son of God, but rather an imposter who deserved contempt for his fraudulent proclamations and ultimate defilement on the cross.[80]

'We went in after him!'

Jim Perry was recalling the most decisive moment of, if not his life, then certainly his years in the parachute regiment.

'We couldn't go to the padre and tell him our mate was play- ing with black magic,' explained Jim. 'We went in after him. That's the way the regiment works. You go in after your mates.'

Jim's friend had read a couple of Dennis Wheatley books and had plunged headlong into the occult, and his consequent actions placed him in real danger of being drummed out of the regiment.

'We bought some books on the subject ourselves,' Jim said, explaining how he and another paratrooper went in after their mate. 'We made a few choice artefacts, set them out in a nearby wood, and we scared the hell out of him. He never went near it again—but we got hooked.'

It was 1964. Jim was nineteen and for the next fifteen years he became a devil-worshipping satanist.

'I did the worst possible thing,' Jim told me as we chatted between seminars at one of the Spring Harvest gatherings at Skegness. 'Jokingly, I made a little voodoo doll of a sergeant who was a pain in the neck, and stuck a big pin it. Seven days later the man had gone. We thought there must be something in this. It was too much of a coincidence. We got involved, at first, through books.'

Soon the written word was inadequate. They joined a small coven off camp at Tidworth, 'mostly sexual thrill seekers, what I call Wallies of the witchcraft world; voyeurs who like to see people with no clothes on'. But there were also the serious occult students.

'We met a satanist who told us to come with him if we wanted to see real power,' added Jim. He and his friend began to be taught a bible with a different perspective than the one that ruled his Sunday school days. In this version, Satan was the 'good guy—the light-bearer in the Garden of Eden'. This was the Satan who had taken Jesus up to a high mountain to offer him the kingdoms of the world, thereby 'proving that he was the god of this world'. This was a Satan who revealed himself in many disguises, one of which was Set, the Egyptian horror god. The group in which Jim became involved was called The Brotherhood. More of Set and The Brotherhood comes later in our study of modern satanists.

Jim's occult study bridged the years into civvy street. Aleister Crowley's books turned him into a hermit, 'for Crowley's magic is a solitary practice'. Jim, now with London

Transport and heading for a supervisor's job, began to progress through the various satanic grades, starting as a neophite (beginner) and climbing towards adept (one who is skilled). In the form of satanism which Jim was following, an occultist had to cross the abyss to become an adept.

'I was working towards the effort of crossing the pit,' explained Jim. 'If you fail, you can bounce right back and lose all the powers you have gained up to that point, or secondly, you can fall into the pit, and then it's goodbye world! While I was training, some strange people moved into the house (sub-divided into flats and bed-sits). Things started to go wrong. I found I couldn't do the tarot readings any more; the crystal ball didn't work, nor did the I Ching [Chinese divination with sticks]. I discovered I was surrounded by Christians.'

A period of spiritual stagnation followed, and what he then believed to be a series of 'unhelpful' events began to occur in his life. For a start, Jim returned to his old love of country and western music and put on the Johnny Cash record *A Believer Sings the Truth*.

'I was too idle to get up again and switch it off after the first good track,' said Jim. 'It was rubbishy Christian music, but then it got to track four and 'He's Alive'. I found myself living what had happened. I must have played it sixty-odd times in the next few days.'

Then there was Veronica, one of the newly-arrived neighbours. She was a gentle, quiet lass who called herself a born-again Christian, and shyly invited him to 'bring his doubts to QPR', the Luis Palau mission in a London football stadium.

'Because of the break in my spiritual life, it seemed that Satan had turned his back on me,' said Jim. 'I didn't realise up to that point what a hold he had over me. The following day, I felt I was being called back home. I got out the tarot cards and it came out nonsense. I tried the crystal ball—all I got was a nice reflection. I had seen the face of Satan through this ball in the past. Now—nothing! I tried everything, even candle magic (looking through the flame in a darkened room and calling up images for guidance). It was only when I got to Queen's Park that I saw the face of Satan gloating over the stadium. Then the congregation stood up and began praising the Lord and the face just began to melt away and I began to realise that maybe he wasn't the god of this world after all. It was 10th July 1984, and I went down onto the pitch to see what this new Lord was like. But the counsellor was hopeless, and the moment passed. And yet I had glimpsed a new power, a new reality, and I wanted it. Later that night at home, I tried to tell Satan to get out of my life. All I could say was the name. I then managed to shout out, "Satan, get behind me." The curtains in the room wafted; a plaque that had been on the wall for years fell to the floor; the door slammed and I felt a great weight lift off me.'

For Jim, it was the beginning of a new life with a new Spirit, though he was to need much counselling and help. For Veronica it was the beginning of six months of depression. It was only later, as they compared their stories, that they recognised this was no coincidence. They found one more thing—a growing affection and love for each other which blossomed into a happy marriage.

Roots of modern satanism

The story that led Jim into fifteen years of hell began, according to the Bible, at the dawn of time in a garden called Eden, and continues to unfold to this day. We could time-travel back to any stage of history and meet satanists in one form or another.

Stepping out of our time capsule in Ancient Britain 300 years before the time of Jesus Christ, we would meet those who were into ritual sacrifice and were responsible for the demise of Pete Marsh, the name the press gave to the well-preserved corpse discovered in 1984 in Lindow Moss, near Wilmslow, Cheshire.[81]

Crossing the channel to France, we would find that human sacrifice was as acceptable as our offering of harvest fruit today. Such sacrifices were necessary to provide the 'priests' and politicians of the day with fresh human entrails by which to divine the signs of the times and the future.

Climbing back into our time capsule, we could zoom forward to various points in our history, meeting Druids or the village wise ones, witnessing the long drawn out battle between paganism and Christianity, perhaps crying with shame at the terrible inquisitions and politics which sent many a poor innocent peasant to the gallows or village ducking stool.

In the dark days, Christianity became so perverse in the hands of superstitious politicians or power-mad, torture-happy clerics that the ordinary peasant often had much more sympathy for those who were their victims.

'The more extreme the government became in using torture on the peasants in the name of saving the country from witches, the greater the sympathy the practitioners of the black arts received,' write Ted Schwarz and Duane Empey in *Satanism*.

So many innocent people were torn apart in the name of justice that all accusations were considered to be fraudulent until proven otherwise. As a result, the ancestors of the early Druids, who were still practising ritual sacrifice, the making of magic potions, and similar actions, remained hidden. They were protected by the same peasants who would have feared them had the government been less zealous in using equally horrible methods to maintain popular support.

In the Dark Ages of our nation, and especially towards the turn of the first millennium when Satan was expected to have his final fling before the Second Coming of Christ, witchcraft began to be especially feared by the Establishment. Even afterwards, when priests and peasants alike realised that they had got their end-of-the-world sums wrong, the battle continued.

A notion began to spread that the devil and demons could do nothing without the aid of humans. People also began to believe that demons could have intimate relations with humans, and there is a record of one woman, Angela de la Barthe, enjoying sex with demons and even having mothered a monster through this process. She then wrote of using other babies to feed her offspring. Thomas Aquinas and Bonaventura had much to say against this type of practice.

Not a pleasant subject. However, these are the roots of the modern-day satanism which affected Jim Perry and continue to influence many others today.

By 1484 and the Bull of Pope Innocent VIII, a full technical definition of witch and warlock had been drawn up:

> Many persons of both sexes, unmindful of their own salvation and straying from the Catholic Faith, have abandoned themselves to devils, incubi and succubi and by their incantations, spells and conjurations and other accursed charms and crafts, enormities and horrid offences, have slain infants yet in the womb, as also the off-spring of cattle, have blasted the produce of the earth, the grapes of the vine, the fruit of the trees, nay men, women, beasts of burden, herd-beasts, as well as animals of other kind, with terrible and piteous pains and sore diseases, both internal and external; they hinder men from performing their sexual act, and women from conceiving, whence husbands cannot know their wives, nor wives receive their husbands; over and above this they blasphemously renounce the Faith which is theirs by the Sacrament of Baptism, and at the instigation of the Enemy of Mankind, they do not shrink from committing and perpetrating the foulest abominations and filthiest excesses to the deadly peril of their own souls, whereby they outrage the Divine Majesty and are a cause of scandal and danger to the very many.

Understandably, this led to witch hunts which were still going on as late as the eighteenth century. The level of false accusations became so bad at one time that a certain gentleman by the name of Ronald Scot protested:

> The fables of witchcraft have taken so fast hold and deepe root in the heart of man, that fewe or non can (nowadaies) with patience indure the hand or correction of God...Such faithlesse people (I saie) are also persuaded that neither haile nor snowe, thunder not lightening, raine not tempestuous winds come from heavens at the commandment of God: but are raised by the cunning and power of witches and conjurers insomuch as a clap of thunder, or a gale of wind is no sooner heard, but either they run to ring the bells, or crie out to burne witches...But if all the divels in hell were dead, and all the witches in England were burnt or hanged; I warrant you we should not faile to have raine, haile and tempests, as we now have, according to the appointment and will of God.

The public institution of Christianity, and certainly its demonology, seemed to be governed by politics, peasant superstition or sadists in sequinned clerical robes. True Christianity—governed by men and women in touch with a less earthly kingdom—retreated into the monasteries.

The basis of true Christianity, the Bible, seems to have been of little import to those in the public religious arena. We need to refresh our memories concerning the biblical teachings, for it was the reversal of these, through a host of heretics and power-hungry politicians and priests, that was to create modern-day satanism.

The biblical Satan

In Bible-based Christianity, the devil, demons and the like are real. Try to dismiss them as myths or characters created to personify evil and you could have a marathon paper chase with the discarded pages of Scripture. It is hard to find a page on which the devil, demons or evil do not feature, either implicitly or explicitly. From Adam to the last amen, Satan is the 'falling star' of Scripture, and almost every writer is inspired to speak against his abode, his effects, his activities and his purposes.

Satan was certainly no myth as far as the Son of God was concerned. It would be difficult to dismiss as a figment of your imagination a devil who lifts you to the roof of the Temple, or whisks you high onto a mountain top (Matthew 4). Jesus' main mission was to destroy the works of the evil one (1 John 3:8), and to drive out the prince of this world by his victorious death on Calvary (John 12:31-32). He even taught his disciples to ask for deliverance from the evil one (Matthew 6:13), gave them authority to cast out demons (Matthew 10:1), and spoke of the time he saw Satan fall from heaven (Luke 10:17f). Jesus took the devil seriously.

The Bible makes it clear that men and women are flawed because they originally became satanists (followers of the serpent in Genesis 3). The Bible further insists that all humans are naturally satanists at heart, wanting to eat according to their own menu rather than God's.

Each individual can cry out with Paul the apostle: 'I do not understand what I do. For what I want to do I do not do, but what I hate I do' (Romans 7:15).

Scripture here is backed up by the reality of life. Nero's tutor Seneca, for instance, said: 'All my life I have been seeking to climb out of the pit of my besetting sins, and I cannot do it; and I never will unless a hand is let down to draw me up.' Mark Twain wrote: 'Man is the only animal that blushes—or needs to!' Tennyson yearned for a better Tennyson in his poetry:

> Ah for a man to arise in me
> That the man I am, may cease to be.

Resolutions are made and unmade often in the same day. Temptation is cunning and clever, devious and deceitful. The

Bible makes crystal clear the identity of the tempter. Sometimes he comes as an angel of light (2 Corinthians 11:14) and at other times like a roaring lion (1 Peter 5:8). He is a liar and false prophet (2 Peter 2:1; 2 Corinthians 11:13).

Developing the devil's *modus operandi*, the Bible places him as head of a universal consortium. He is not almighty, and does not possess the attributes of being in all places at once, nor of having all knowledge. He was created Lucifer, the brightest object of God's creation (as implied in Luke 10:18 and Revelation 9:1 and 12:9). Following his fall from heaven he became, among other things, Beelzebub, the prince of demons (Matthew 12:24f; Mark 3:20f), and therefore it is appropriate to describe demons as his subjects or agents. A hierarchy of demons is implied in the descriptions of 'rulers...authorities...powers of this dark world...spiritual forces [agents] of evil in the heavenly realms' (Ephesians 6:12). There is an implication that evil spirits are delegated to oversee cities and nations, and to delay or prevent the Lord's work being done in them (Daniel 10:12f).

Perhaps this is being far too complimentary to hell's demons. Organisation and efficiency do not appear to be their strongest attributes. To understand this, we need to consider their origins.

There are many references in the Bible to the fall of Satan and the angels who side with him (Revelation 12:9; Job 4:18b; Matthew 25:41; 2 Peter 2:4). There are implications that a third of the angels were swept out of heaven along with the devil (Revelation 12:4,9; Daniel 8:10). We have to be careful not to take the poetic sections of Scripture too literally, but Bible scholars over the centuries have deemed it safe to state, at the very least, that there was a heavenly war in which the losing minority were punished with exile. We can further assume, with safety, that those in opposition to God were not the most selfless of beings. We would still not be exaggerating to say that they were out to grab power, to seize control, to steal what was

not theirs. They must still be selfish, undisciplined, disobedi-
ent, liars, thieves, rebels and generally the last recruits you
would dream of enlisting. Despite this, Scripture makes it clear
that the devil is powerful, and so are his forces, and even God's
beings treat them with a measure of respect (Jude 9).

The work of the demons can be so damaging, states Scripture, that spirits should be tested to discern whether they are
good or bad (1 Corinthians 12:3; 1 Timothy 4:1). The bad spirit
is unable to acknowledge the lordship of Christ, though it will
hide this in devious ways. Scripture states that the apostle Peter
thought he was on the right spiritual lines when he offered to
defend Jesus against all-comers. He was amazed when Jesus
turned on him and said:

'Get behind me, Satan! You are a stumbling-block to me;
you do not have in mind the things of God, but the things of
men' (Matthew 16:23).

At least some of the demons have personalities and a high
degree of intelligence. Many recognised Jesus and declared
him to be the Son of God (Mark 3:11f). They communicated
with each other (Matthew 12:43f), and they shudder because of
God (James 2:19). On one occasion an evil spirit even dis-
cerned that the seven sons of Sceva were false exorcists and
attacked them: 'Jesus I know, and I know about Paul, but who
are you?' (Acts 19:13f). The sons were given such a severe
beating that they ran away naked and bleeding.

Demons can invade and possess (Matthew 17:18f), deceive
(2 Corinthians 4:4), injure and attempt murder (Mark 9:25-27),
perform miracles and incite to war (Revelation 16:14), and
cause drunkenness, epilepsy, blindness and deformity
(Matthew 9:32; 17:15; 12:22). One of their chief aims is to lead
people away from the faith (1 Timothy 4:1). As a cautionary
note, I add the observation that the devil and demons are not the
only cause of the above. Scripture stresses that the world and
the flesh are just as culpable.

The unbiblical Satan

Tracing the rise (and rise) of the heretical Satan since the time of Christ is fascinating yet sad. It began with those who believed that the way to salvation lay in possessing some secret knowledge (Gnostics). Almost invariably this involved believing that there were two independent and separate forces: God who was in charge of the spiritual, and an evil entity responsible for matter.

A Persian called Mani takes us one step further. He claimed that he had the final revelation, 200 years after the death and resurrection of Christ. He and his followers (Manichaeans) believed that there was light and darkness, which existed separately in eternity.

This directly contradicted the Bible, which plainly stated that dualism (two separate universal powers) was impossible when there was only one God (one almighty power). True, God delegated some of his power to the accuser (Satan), but even that could only be exercised with permission (Job 1:6-12).

Within four centuries, the Manichaeans were in retreat, making way for a new group of heretics—the Paulicians. These accepted only Paul's letters and the Gospels as the written word of God. Their founder, Constantine, taught that the God of heaven hated all material things, and this meant that those parts of Scripture which stated that God had made the earth, like the Old Testament, must be the work of an evil deity who himself was the creator and god of this world. Despite persecution, the Paulicians survived mainly in Armenia into the last century, and one of their offshoots takes us one more step closer to our goal of understanding modern-day satanism.

A priest named Bogomil took over a movement started by the Paulicians in what is now Bulgaria. Around the turn of the first millennium, he taught that the evil deity of the Paulicians was in fact the first son of God, the proud and independent

Satanael. This deity was expelled and promptly set up business for himself, creating a new heaven and earth, in which he placed Adam and Eve. Cain was the product of Satanael and Eve and was the cause of much evil on earth. God eventually sent his second son, Jesus, to overcome Satanael on the cross. The Bogomiles disowned the sacraments of baptism and Holy Communion as satanic rites because material symbols were used.

Bogomilism was not a long-term success, largely due to the reluctance of most followers to indulge in sex and marriage. Their only lasting procreation was a few offshoot heresies, including the Cathari, and Albigensians (named after the town of Albi in Southern France).

The Albigensians had a New Testament god of light (truth and spirit) and an Old Testament god of darkness (error and material), and mankind was caught in the crossfire. The good Albigensians worked to purify themselves from material things like marriage, sex and food (though vegetarianism was just about permitted). Obviously, they were not destined for a great reign, even less so when they murdered the Pope's representative in the thirteenth century. A papal crusade wiped them out, but not before bequeathing one or two key beliefs to others. Hell, they believed, did not really exist. Hell was when the soul was imprisoned in the wicked body. Some souls decided to enjoy themselves a little too much in their hell, and orgies became a way of life. The leaders consequently began to teach that those who were not saved into the spirit world went deeper into the material world, and their souls were transmigrated into the bodies of lower animals. This can be linked possibly to later ideas of witches having familiars (personalities or spirits possessing dogs, cats and other animals).

By this point in history, a dual system of two gods (a goody and a baddy) was well established in Western cultural thinking. It was against this background that things turned sour for a group who called themselves the Poor Fellow-Soldiers of

Christ and the Temple of Solomon. They were more famously known as...

The Knights Templar

They were 'Poor' because of their vow of poverty. They were chaste and obedient 'Fellow-Soldiers of Christ' because these military men had set up a religious order to help and protect pilgrims en route to the Holy Land. They belonged to the 'Temple of Solomon' because that was the part of the king's palace in Jerusalem where they were billeted. These warrior-knights with monastic vows wore the famous white mantle emblazoned with a crusader's red cross over their chain-mail.

The Knights were set up in about 1120 by Hugo des Payens, a knight from Burgundy, and Godfrey of St Omer, from Northern France, and developed into three ranks: the knights who joined for life, the sergeants, mainly of the wealthy bourgeois who joined for set terms, and chaplains who took life-long vows to perform religious services for the Knights.

One practice and one event brought a gradual deterioration in the values and standards of the Knights. The first was the habit of accepting gifts from the grateful, especially from the wealthy and landed pilgrims. The donations created a great treasury and with this came growing political influence and corruption. However, the event which clearly spelled doom for the Templars came in 1291, when pilgrims were turned away from Jerusalem and all Christians were expelled from the Holy Land. Almost overnight, the Knights had lost their crusading function, and the Templars were reduced to counting their gold, wondering what to do with the rest of their lives.

They did not have long to wait. The king of a bankrupt France, Philip IV, saw the Knights Templar as his way to solvency. He cleverly engineered the dissolution of the Knights, by applying political pressure to the Pope in Rome, commandeered their wealth and, in the process, got rid of an independent and increasingly secret society which occasionally ruffled the throne. One of the most effective ways of destroying the order was to charge 120 Templars, including Grand Master Jacques de Molay, with heresy, witchcraft and sodomy. Despite protestations of innocence, they were duly executed. At least this is one version. Schwarz and Empey give another aspect. They write of the Templars,

> They lost faith in the Catholic church; they wanted wealth, fame and glory, none of which seemed to come from serving pilgrims. A number of members decided that the answer was to look to the opposition. If worshipping God failed to help them reach their desires, perhaps Satan would be more responsive. Their ceremonies would be on the same date as those of the Catholic church, but they would reverse all the rituals...An investigation in 1307 revealed that members engaged in strange rituals, some of which eventually became the basis for voodoo and satanic worship...The Knights Templar did not believe that Christ was the Son of God, but rather an imposter who deserved contempt for his fraudulent proclamations and ultimate defilement on the cross.'[83]

There is just one more step to take before we arrive at the modern form of satanism which enthralled people like Jim Perry and still keeps many others in its grasp today.

The Black Mass

This one ritual perhaps sums up the horror of what happened next. It came to symbolise a revolt against the rottenness of the established order of the fourteenth and fifteenth centuries.

Had we lived in France at that time, we might easily have found ourselves attending the Black Mass rather than one of the corrupt, pre-Reformation church services. It was an age which echoed with the screams from those on the Inquisition racks, and the fear of thumbscrews drove many underground. One way of getting back at the bloody, cruel regime was to mock or reverse everything that it stood for, and the Mass and its Catholic teachings, which were at the very heart of French society, became the peasant satanists' targets.

It was, I believe, a small though fairly impotent forerunner to the great French Revolution that was to follow 200 years later. The ordinary people in parts of France took great delight in desecrating communion chalices and hosts. They used naked women as altars, trampled on the cross and turned Good Friday into a day of orgies. They turned the Black Mass into as rigid a ritual as that practised in the Catholic Church, and this was passed through the underground network so that the variety of protesting groups could join in. Of course, it was not purely protest. It was also a great excuse to practise as much perversion as they liked. Schwarz and Empey report:

> Sex acts of all manner had to be performed by the cult members. Rituals required that human and animal blood be tasted by participants. When a human was put to death, the still warm heart had to be removed…Perversion after perversion became ritual in a religion as structured as that which was practised with the church.[84]

There were reliable reports at this time of pregnant women offering their babies for sacrifice to Satan; of other children going missing; of satanic acts which left trails of death and torture as the nation itself became more satanic than Catholic. Eventually, there was a public backlash. Trials and vigilante groups began to drive satanism underground and many satanists fled to other countries—including England.

As we have already noted in Chapter 3 England had its own history of witchcraft and the occult, and satanism was to become yet another strand for a growing alternative underground society.

8

Satanism Today

A satanist may be, and often is, an assassin, a warrior, an out-law—in real life. The imitation satanists, however, pretend to be these things—their fantasy-life is greater than their real experiences of such things.[85]

The wheels rattled across a cattle grid, and I changed down into first gear to begin a long, slow climb into the mini alps of the Long Mynd above Church Stretton in Shropshire. I was heading for a meeting with what I had been promised was "real satanism".

As I drove, the coming encounter took my breath away almost as much as the sheer drop beside what was becoming little more than a mountain-goat track graced with tarmac. My destination was Pole Cottage—actually a black, corrugated-iron shed no bigger than the average living room, so the locals had said. Outside it, I was to meet Christos Beest—at least that's all he was prepared to sign himself when replying to my letters enquiring into the satanic Order of the Nine Angles (ONA).

The satanists I had met prior to this—either ministering to those on their way out, evangelising those within or interview-

ing the leaders of various covens, temples, grottoes or lodges—
were located in towns and cities, and surrounded by lots of
reassuring buildings and normal non-satanic people.

The track levelled out among the moorland peaks with a toy-
town Church Stretton nestling a thousand feet below, and, as if
at the command of some Hollywood horror-movie director, the
mist began to roll in. Thankfully, it was barely 10 o'clock on an
August Saturday morning, but even so I worried whether the
precautions I had taken would be sufficient.

The lone Church Stretton police constable—Dave, a reassur-
ingly down-to-earth bobby who knew the area better than most
after his twenty-year stint in the village—had called in rein-
forcements in the form of a detective constable.

'We've two pair of high-powered binoculars in here,' he
drawled in a homely Shropshire-lad accent as he held aloft a
well-used rucksack. 'You won't be out of sight for a moment.'

We had all taken this meeting seriously, for each of us had
read the order's literature—*Fenrir, Journal of the Sinister*. A
special edition of the magazine had been sent to me anony-
mously after the showing of a television programme based on
my last book about the New Age. A note affixed to the front of
the magazine was unsigned, but the sender explained that an
office colleague had left it lying around during a lunch break.
He or she thought something should be done about its contents.
The following extracts show why:

> The hard reality of satanism is that it is very different from both the
> media image pedalled by imitation satanists in both Europe and
> America...

> Satanism involves sacrifice...first because it is a test of satanic
> character...second, it has magickal benefits...third, it sorts the
> imitation or toy satanists out from the genuine...

The actual sacrifice has two forms: (1) during a ritual; (2) by practical means (e.g. assassination/'accidents')...death will seldom if ever be seen as a satanic act even if it has occurred during ritual...execution of this act is an essential prerequisite to Adeptship...

Satanic sacrifice makes a contribution to improving the human stock, removing the worthless, the weak, the diseased (in terms of character)...Mostly, they are dross whose removal will aid change/the growth of civilization/the Aeonic imperative.[86]

As I drove towards Pole Cottage, I remember trying to lighten my thoughts by contemplating where Christian writers ranked on the satanic scale of victims. Would it aid change to rid the satanic civilisation of a nosy vicar? Reading some of the order's other material made a sense of humour less appropriate.

In the *Fenrir* version of the ONA Black Mass, the celebrant is told where to stand during sex and blood rituals. The sex could be with a baby, a young child, a teenager, an adult or a dead body, and the blood could be from an animal or human sacrifice. The fat of babies, sometimes even unborn babies, was prescribed for certain anointing oils and unguents. Human fat was required to mix with pitch and other ingredients to produce the traditional satanic black candles.

Surely this was all the product of a diseased, juvenile imagination! Surely all I would find at Pole Cottage would be an extreme right-wing bigot in bovver boots whose skinhead was as much bereft of intelligence as hair!

In more reasonable moments, I knew that there was nothing 'sure' about anything connected to this satanic order. The *Fenrir* journals were well-produced, with good grammar (except for the odd split infinitive) and perfect spelling. I had discovered that the journals ran to three volumes and dated back to 1958, which put them beyond the realms of a practical joke.

They were written by people who had a university-level grasp of philosophy and religions, and I took it seriously enough to travel to the heart of England in search of the truth.

Village bobby Dave had an additional reason for treating it soberly. He, together with half a dozen other police forces across the country, were at that time in the middle of a year-long investigation into what looked like ritual slashing and ceremonial blood-letting of horses. Dave had had three such cases to investigate, each of the horses having had the genital areas badly lacerated.

I was almost past Pole Cottage before I recognised it through a thickening mist. 'So much for the police binoculars,' I thought, and wondered which bits of shrubbery the two policemen were hiding behind. There did not seem to be any in view that were large enough to cover a brace of well-built officers. I pulled up beside a man in his mid-twenties, dressed as a hiker and seated on the stile in front of the black corrugated hut. We shook hands, introduced ourselves and began a conversation which seemed as normal as a Saturday morning chat on the vicarage lawn.

This was Christianity meeting satanism face-to-face and, initially, there was not much trust evident on either side. I did not tell Christos about the two police officers, and he did not tell me about his associates whom I suspected were somewhere around. It was not until later, during a de-briefing back at Church Stretton police station, that my suspicions were confirmed by one of the officers who had maintained constant surveillance of one of Christos' friends during the interview.

The lack of trust seemed to lessen as we began to relax on a couple of logs outside the black shed. Our curiosity about each other drove the conversation towards understanding. For my part, I wanted solutions to a bewildering array of questions. How could Christos and his fellow satanists—'university professors, teachers, scientists and other professionals'—talk at

one moment about a new aeonic; a new age and a new world
order, and then in the next moment condone human sacrifice?
How could this seemingly sensitive, gentle musician and artist
be a spokesman for child sacrifice? It seemed a reasonable
place to start:

Me: What is your kind of satanism about? What are you
          really aiming for?
Christos: It's like a chess game, moving pieces to create rip-
          ples in the fabric of time...with a view to creating a
          new civilisation. We're actually coming to the end of
          the Western civilisation...historians have devised a
          model of history showing how each civilisation
          grew, changed and then decayed, and they all lasted
          an aeon, 1,500 years. A new civilisation emerges
          from the ashes of the old...We're actually doing
          things now to enable the next civilisation to come
          about.
Me: Human sacrifices? Are these merely ripples?
Christos: Yes. The theory is that if there are certain people that
          are detrimental to...creating a new type of society,
          their removal aids the emergence of that. That's why
          wars are quite important in that respect, or the assas-
          sination of politicians...It's not just killing for the
          sake of killing...It's something that's very ratio-
          nal...Contrary to public opinion, it's never a virgin,
          or a down-and-out. It's always somebody of whom
          people would say that he or she deserved it.

I challenged him about the order's own admission that sex and
sacrifice involved the young. Who would dare to say that toddlers and babies deserved death? Christos immediately dis-
tanced himself from these views, claiming that each of the journal's writers, and indeed each satanist, was responsible for his

or her own views and actions. He explained that satanism was
nothing if not individualistic. Personally, he abhorred the sacrifice and abuse of children, though apparently his abhorrence
was not quite strong enough to make him disown those who
did. I wondered about adult sacrifice.

Me: Your journal states that your sacrifices are often
           made to look like accidents. Have you ever done
           that?

Christos: Well, if I had, I wouldn't admit it, would I? Though
           you've probably met quite a few who have admitted
           it.

Me: The vast majority of satanists I meet throw their
           hands up in horror when I mention sacrifice. They
           claim that sacrificing babies and human beings is a
           figment of gutter press fantasy.

Christos: Oh, well there's certainly a few leather-clad, heavy-
           metal characters who say they've killed one or two
           people...Do you sense that I would be capable of
           killing somebody?

Me: Not at all.

Christos: Right. So maybe you've got your answer then.

Me: I'm not a perfect judge of a character.

We turned to the sort of civilisation which the satanists were
striving to introduce. Would it be right to assume there was a
strong element of the Nazi élitism involved? Would it be unfair
to ask if today's satanists would feel at home running a modern
gas chamber for what they believed to be the dross of society?

Christos: We ought to get back to the old pagan ethos of explo-
           ration...going out to new frontiers...having that
           forward-looking society and not the morbid inward-
           looking, apathetic, self-obsessed, ill-disciplined

society...one which is similar to the Vikings...recaptur- ing the human spirit...which is why National Socialism is often used by satanists because that is really one of only a few political forms which enshrines that idea. We don't necessarily believe in these extreme right-wing Nazi groups, but we do think they can be used to bring about change and a new order.

Me: Where does Satan come into all this? Is he real to you?

Christos: I regard him as a militant personification of nature itself...an adversarial energy, the accuser; somebody who contradicts the norm in order to create conflict, and via conflict to create change...a very creative, positive form of destruction.

Me: If I was talking to another ONA-er, would I get a similar answer?

Christos: It would depend on the individual member...some regard Satan as a lover or as a brother, but never a master; never something that you bow down to or worship. It's something that you seek guidance from, and then maybe eventually become Satan yourself.

It was at about this time in our interview that a blue Sierra glided slowly by us for the third time. In such a desolate wilderness where any wheeled traffic was a major event, it was screamingly obvious that the driver was a plain-clothes officer—well, at least it was screamingly obvious to me. It was only later at the debriefing that I learned that, because of the mist, this had been the only way Dave could occasionally keep me in his sights.

Christos, if he did notice, chose to ignore it. Being a good citizen and hating to waste police time, I wished there was some way of signalling that I was not now to be an item on the weekend satanic menu. Christos and I had already agreed, surprisingly, that vicars and writers did have their redeeming points. Vicars, apparently, caused people to think, and this could aid change. Satanists would do their own fine tuning to the changes at a later stage in the evolution of the new order. When the blue Sierra started on its fourth glide-by, I began to bring our conversation to a close.

I was still curious as to why Christos and his ONA-ers had insisted on being viewed as 'real satanists'. What was wrong with other groups such as the more public Church of Satan and the Temple of Set? These (which we cover in the next chapter) had looked quite satanic enough for me when I had investigated them. But not so for Christos.

Christos: I think it's important that these groups are exposed for what they are. Certainly the Temple of Set is run very much like a religion...Aquino [the leader] claims an infernal mandate (from Satan himself) which gives him authority over others...which is something very dangerous. That's not at all the spirit of satanism. He's distorting it. In fact he's destroying the anarchic aspect of it, the self, the liberating aspect of it.

The ONA's journal was even more vicious in its criticism of the Church of Satan and the Temple of Set.

Satanism is hard and very dangerous. This danger is much more than just a mental or a psychic one of a kind sometimes experienced in magickal workings. It is a personal danger of the life-and-death kind. If it is not, then it is not tough enough, it is not satanic.

For far too long the pathetic, imitation Satanists, such as those in the Temple of Set and the Church of Satan, have had no one to contradict their sickly, wimpish versions of Satanism—they have tried to deny the darkness and evil which are essential to Satanism because the frauds in those organisations are fundamentally weak; they have never gone to their limits, never experienced the realness of evil.

They have tried to make Satanism safe and respectable: they have intellectualized it because they are typical products of this present intellectualized, peace-loving, we-need-to-be-safe society. A Satanist is like a beast of prey—*in real life*, not in fantasy. A Satanist may be, and often is, an assassin, a warrior, an outlaw—*in real life*. The imitation Satanists, however, pretend to be these things—their fantasy-life is greater than their real experiences of such things.

In our next chapter, you will be able to judge for yourselves whether these are mere petulant playground jibes, or an accurate assessment of the more public side of satanism.

9

The Public Face of Satanism

We perform human sacrifices by proxy…[87]

OR…

Satanism, represented by the Church of Satan, philosophically condemns such practices as…sacrifice…as can be seen in…The Satanic Bible by our founder and High Priest, Anton Szandor LaVey.[88]

The day satanism went public on Walpurgisnacht, 30th April–1st May 1966,[89] was the day the world began to sit up and take notice of a former circus musician, lion-tamer and self-publicist, Anton Szandor LaVey. This was the night he shaved his head bald—a traditional power-raising ritual for black magicians—and inaugurated the First Church of Satan in what he declared to be 'Anno Santanas'—Year One of Satan's reign.

At first glance, it seems that there may be something in Christos' accusations about the play-acting of toy-satanists. He is certainly not the only satanist or occultist to dismiss LaVey's enterprise as a satanic circus. Fifteen years after the first public satanic services, many leading members revolted against their 'Black Pope' for making light of their religion, and formed themselves into the Temple of Set. It was to be one of many splinter groups, some of which still exist today.

Both the Church of Satan and the Temple of Set have followings in England, and both publish literature for British members. The Church of Satan has a voice in an A5-size, blue periodical issued by the Society of the Dark Lily, and the temple has an official magazine, *The Scroll of Set*, plus *The Black Pyramid*, usually used as the voice of the high priest to the membership. The temple also has its own British Magister in the form of David Austen, who lives in Lewisham, London.

The biggest headache for any researcher into satanism is locating the truth, for this does not appear to be a natural attribute for those in the midst of what is often a venomous circle of curses and counter-curses. What is certain is that the Church of Satan did attract a significant following in the believe-anything State of California. Just how many, depends on who is to be believed. One source put it as high as 50,000 card-carrying satanists with 'several millions of sympathetic non-members waiting in the wings', while another guess was 'never higher than 300...with a 30 per cent turnover per year'.[90]

There is one fact about the membership that is known: it rightfully boasted a colourful array of San Francisco socialites, influential property owners, European nobility, American heiresses and a plethora of showbiz people like Jayne Mansfield and, for a time, Sammy Davis Jnr.

As we look at other known facts, it would seem that there was more than just circus sawdust and showmanship in the make-up of Anton LaVey. The formation of his character and values began with whispered tales of vampires and black magic at the knee of his Transylvanian gypsy grandmother. It continued in his Hungarian parents' home in gangland Chicago, where characters called Bugsy, Mickey and Al peppered each conversation with phrases like, *'Cui bono?'*—(who gains?). Young Anton was fed on the milk of human greed and reared in the cynicism of the 'racket' in which everybody had an 'angle', even the church ('especially the church, 'cos nobody's supposed to know it's a racket').[91] Present from the earliest days, therefore, were the seeds of satanism—looking after 'numero uno', the caricatured hypocrisy of God and religion, and a yearning for some 'Transylvanian' power to survive in a blood-sucking society.

Later, there were other, still more formative influences. A brief look at these not only helps paint a picture of our first public satanist, but it also bridges the geography and years since the seventeenth century French Black Mass in Chapter 7.

The Black Order of Satanists

Blanche Barton, writer of the official history *The Church of Satan*, tells of the startling impact on fifteen-year-old Anton when he was among the first to view confiscated Nazi *Schauer-filmen* (horror films) at a Berlin command post in the spring of 1945. At the time, Anton was accompanying his civilian engineer uncle who was on hire to the army. The films featured the Black Order of Satanists which existed during, and influenced greatly, the Third Reich. The films' stories were fictional, but the details of the Black Order and its rituals were all too real. Through this and subsequent studies, young Anton began to learn how the satanists were linked with another occult group entitled...

The Thule Society

This was a pagan-satanic group for German professional classes and high-ranking army officers, and this, together with the Order of New Templars (based to some extent on the first Knights Templar) was to prove a great influence on ascending politicians like Heinrich Himmler and Adolph Hitler. It was a Thule member, dentist Friedrich Krohn, who provided Hitler with the symbol for his newly-formed National Socialist Party in the twenties. This member suggested the shape of a crooked

Sanskrit cross called '*Su asti*' (swastika) meaning 'good', and Hitler took to it immediately. However, he made one slight adjustment by reversing the crooked ends of the arms so that they pointed to the left. This spoke volumes to Krohn and other Thule members: reversing the ends also reversed its meaning from 'good' to 'evil'. What was to become the Nazi emblem was in fact a symbol to invoke the satanic.

It was Thule's satanic-type thinking which encouraged Hitler towards the Final Solution for the Jews. The society had long believed that the Jews of the world were secretly conspiring to take power, and were using their own hidden powers and secret rituals to bring this about. Thule hit back magically with the help of masonic and Nordic rituals, and Hitler decided to add a little something extra—gas chambers. The Thules and Templars also united to encourage Hitler in his plans to establish a super race of ruthless Aryans.

A young Anton LaVey took it all on board as he planned his future.

The Hell Fire Club

The thin black line of satanism running back through history was LaVey's next study. He learned much, for instance, from the Hell Fire Club which played a large part in transferring satanism from France to America via the high society of eighteenth century England.

This was a satanic club modelled on the debauchery and orgiastic feasting that had all but been drummed out of France during the Revolution. The French peasant classes rose up in part because they were sick of being used, abused and sacrificed by the rich aristocracy, and Madame Guillotine was not only justice, but their sweet revenge. Not so in England where revolution was probably averted by, among other things, a prior civil war and also the revival of a vibrant and society-changing Christianity, courtesy of John Wesley.

Sir Francis Dashwood set up the Hell Fire Club at the zenith of England's glory. It was almost as though, having conquered the world, the rich swooned with the royals and even the religious in an intoxication of power, and they congregated in subgroups of the Hell Fire Club, with names like "the Blasters" and "the Sons of Midnight". Some modern commentators dismiss them as the inadequate dandies of high society, even though they included the Earl of Sandwich, Charles Churchill, the poet son of the Archbishop of Canterbury, and the Earl of Bute, who was to become Prime Minister. Dashwood was himself to become Chancellor of the Exchequer, boasting one moment about invoking the devil, and the next calling on God as a repentant Christian. His spiritual life see-sawed between the two as he seemed to make genuine efforts to free himself. It appeared to be a losing battle.

Fancy fops the Hell Fire Club devotees may have been, but they and their clubs became so notorious that the king of the day, George I, was forced to issue an edict against 'scandalous societies of young persons who meet together in a most impious and blasphemous manner'. He declared that they had insulted 'the sacred principles of Holy Religion' and were an 'affront' to Almighty God.

It was these clubs, LaVey came to believe, which eventually fed satanism into the American culture. Blanche Barton in her book on the satanic church wrote that LaVey had long maintained that if the people really knew of the Hell Fire Club link, plus the secret beliefs of other early patriots, they might prefer to rename their country the 'United Satanic America'.[92] She explains: 'Benjamin Franklyn's association with Dashwood and other members of the group helped lay the foundations for the emerging nation.'[93]

A little caution is advised here. Ms Barton appears to have a tendency to overstate her case on occasions. For instance, she enrols the Archbishop of Canterbury as a Hell Fire Club member, when in reality the membership belonged to the arch-bishop's poet grandson.

Another formative ingredient in the make-up of LaVey was Rabelais' utopian...

Abbey of Thelema

This nineteenth century establishment, described in Gargantua and Pantagruel as 'less an abbey than a palace of perpetual indulgence',[94] was later to inspire Aleister Crowley who set up his own abbey in Sicily, as we have already noted. Two other groups also influenced LaVey.

The Hollywood Set

This was not its official name, but it would have been appropri-ate. It was a loose collection of Hollywood actors and writers, including W.C. Fields and John Barrymore, 'who took on the names of dark deities and forthrightly paid homage to satanic forces'.[95] Finally, there was...

The Fortean Society

This bunch of sceptics, who still have a sizeable following in this country and abroad, were attracted to Charles Fort and his psychic jaunts between the two world wars. He was fascinated by strange phenomena and spent his life investigating them, and some of his members eventually joined Anton LaVey in his first Magic Circle, a forerunner to his public church.

And so it came to pass that Anton Szandor LaVey felt called upon by the dark forces to create the first public satanic church. And, of course, no church could be without its doctrine, and so *The Satanic Bible*, a black paperback, was published. It promptly jumped into the best-seller lists, soon topping the half-million sales mark, and included the Nine Statements on which the church was founded. These declared that Satan rep-resented:

1. Indulgence instead of abstinence.

2. Vital existence instead of spiritual pipe dreams.

3. Undefiled wisdom instead of hypocritical deceit.

4. Kindness to those who deserve it instead of love wasted on ingrates.

5. Vengeance instead of trying to turn the other cheek.

6. Responsibility for the responsible instead of concern for psychic vampires.

Satan also represents:

7. Man as just another animal, sometimes better, more often worse than those who walk on all fours, who, because of his 'divine spiritual and intellectual development' has become the most vicious animal of them all!

8. All of the so-called sins, as they all lead to physical, mental or emotional gratification.

9. The best friend the church has ever had, as he kept it in business all these years![96]

LaVey claimed that he was ushering in the new satanic Age of Fire, having worked this out with a complicated form of mathematics based on multiples of nine. This age alternated with the Age of Ice, when passions were cool and controlled. The Age of Fire was, of course, the total opposite.

LaVey further taught that the only god was the one that existed between the ears, and, if this was so, then why not make a god which suited man's own image, appetites, emotions and needs? Why create a god that only encouraged feelings of guilt?

Added to this, LaVey taught that life was Darwinian, and only the fittest would survive, and only they would rule. The church's statements of faith had many parallels to those of the Knights Templar, Aleister Crowley and the Golden Dawn with an over-indulgent helping of the Thelemic concept that each follows his own will.

Many have wondered whether LaVey should be taken seriously. Of his brand of satanism there is less doubt, especially in the United States where the impact of satanism has been massive. Hardly a year goes by without some "How to Cope" book being published on the latest ways of keeping kids safe from satanic influences. But about the man there is less certainty.

At one level, he seemed to practise what he preached, whether it was satanically baptising his daughter, Zeena, or burying at sea a naval satanist, complete with full military and satanic honours (the US Navy were constitutionally obliged to assist at the funeral because the Church of Satan was by then a registered and recognised religion).

On another level, LaVey seemed to be a tongue-in-cheek showman, who often played up to the world's stereotype of Satan by appearing in a red devil suit, complete with horns and forked tail. His *Satanic Bible* alternates between the grotesque and the outrageous, and many of its statements are difficult to take too seriously. It is the same with his contradictory comments on human sacrifice.

'We perform human sacrifices by proxy,' LaVey claimed in his book *The Devil Worshippers*.[97] On one occasion he claimed to have placed a death curse on Sam Brody, Jayne Mansfield's lawyer/boyfriend, shortly before he and the actress were killed in a horrific road accident in the second year of his church.[98] However, when I challenged the church on sacrifice, I was given the following contradictory statement contained in a reply to a letter of enquiry sent to me, 'Satanism, represented by the Church of Satan, philosophically condemns such practices as the abuse and sacrifice of children, adult humans and animals as can be seen in the following quotations from *The Satanic Bible* by our founder and High Priest, Anton Szandor LaVey.' There then followed appropriate texts selected from his bible.

How seriously should we take this inconsistent character in

pantomime costume? A picture kept flashing into my mind as I neared the end of my research on the church. I think it is reasonably accurate. It was of Anton LaVey taking his pet 500lb Nubian lion, Togare, walkies in the streets surrounding his thirteen-room, black-painted house in San Francisco, his eyes twinkling mischievously between his bald pate and goatee beard, and his mind delighting at the fearful response of the neighbours. As my last questions on the church were being answered, I got the distinct impression that LaVey still loved to shock, and that satanism had replaced Togare on his walks through society.

A satanic reformation?

There were many breakaways from, or imitations of, the LaVey church by those convinced, for an assortment of reasons, that they could do better. The list, almost impressive enough for the *Guinness Book of Records*, includes the Church of Satanic Brotherhood, Ordo Templi Santanus, Order of the Black Ram, Temple of Set, Church of Lucifer, Shrine of the Little Mother, Church of S.A.T.A.N., the Church of Satan, Order of Baal, the Satanic Church, the Orthodox Satanic Church and, more recently, the Church of Satanic Liberation, Temple of Nepthys, the Brotherhood, the Black Hand, Order of Selohaar, Temple of Amon-Khemu, Coven Cernunnos, Sentinels of Esoteric Thought, Universal Mission of Satan and the Ancient Brotherhood of Satan.

The Church of Satan claims also that other groups have links with them, such as the Werewolf Order, the Abraxas Foundation, Thee Temple ov [sic] Psychic Youth, the Order of Fenris and the Lilith Grotto. However, not all of those would boast of being connected with the Church of Satan.

Some of the above groups have faded away for lack of support or money. Some vanished from the public satanic arena, though they still secretly operate their own isolated brand of satanism. More of these in the next chapter.

Our investigation of the public face of satanism would be incomplete without reference to the acrimonious schism of its first church in 1975, when one of LaVey's priests, Dr Michael A. Aquino, a top-security clearance officer in the United States Army, launched what he believed to be a reformation. He called his movement...

The Temple of Set

The parting of the ways was, and still is, accompanied by harsh words. The Temple of Set published its version of the divorce in *The Crystal Tablet of Set*,[99] and the Church of Satan replied and made counter-accusations in *Pretenders to the Throne*.[100]

The Church of Satan began by claiming that a breakaway involving thirty members could hardly be called a schism, but the Temple of Set countered by insisting that 'the entire priesthood' of the Church of Satan left. Aquino went further and accused LaVey of 'selling degrees':

> A small, stable nucleus of serious and sincere devotees had indeed developed [in the church], but for the most part the Church had served to attract merely fad-followers, egomaniacs, and assorted oddballs whose primary interest in becoming Satanists lay in being able to flash their membership cards for cocktail-party notoriety. Anton decided that the Church might as well be converted to a vehicle for his personal financial benefit, hence in May of 1975 he announced a decision to sell the Satanic Priesthood and all high degrees for funds or objects of value.[101]

LaVey replied that the sale of degrees was merely a redevelopment of the Church of Satan to which Aquino had already agreed at a meeting of the organising council. Aquino scored one of those unanswerable points when he simply announced that Set (a sort of Egyptian version of Satan) had told him to take control of a new church. All LaVey could offer as answer was a bit of name calling, suggesting that Aquino was always 'striving for fancy titles' and that his departure was the 'welcome housecleaning of an element that had become less desirable to the future development of the Church of Satan'. He felt that Aquino's background—'a boyhood steeped in military academies and in pursuit of Boy Scout merit badges'—was a hindrance.

Dr Aquino, however, went on to make two valid criticisms of the Church of Satan, and these were to distance the temple from its 'parent' body.

First, Aquino believed that Set was an actual entity whereas LaVey believed that Satan was merely symbolic; a figure of praise to 'self-interest, indulgence and a glorification of the carnal and material'. Aquino believed that Set was an infernal personality with whom followers could commune. Had he not himself received from Set on the night of 12th June 1975 four hours of dictation, which were eventually published as *The Book of Coming Forth by Night*? This communication informed him that LaVey and his church had forfeited its right to represent the satanic, and that the infernal mantle had now been passed to Aquino. This, more than any other thing, infuriated LaVey and prompted the war of words which still rages as I write.

Secondly, Aquino thought it philosophically odd that satanism would not be able to exist without Christianity, its main opponent! He rightly claimed that the Church of Satan 'could not escape the self-assumed limitation of being anti-Christian'.[102]

The Temple of Set therefore divorced itself from the Satan of Christianity and based itself on ancient Egyptian mythology in which Set was cast as the evil principle by the cults of Osiris and Isis.

So obviously, the new setians would from this point cease to be satanists?

Well, not quite. It seems that despite the divorce, despite this affair with a newer, more academic infernal lover, Dr Aquino could not quite make a clean break. To this day, they continue to be satanists in all but name only. In the temple's 'new enquirers' leaflet, Dr Aquino simply states: 'The Temple of Set enjoys the colorful [sic] legacy of the Black Arts, and we use many forms of historical Satanic imagery for our artistic simulation and pleasure.'[103]

Aquino was challenged over this apparent contradiction in an occult magazine when he was asked why he did not attempt a clean break with the satanist label.

> Our answer is that you might say that satanism is our Old Testament. That's what we grew out of. We have a traditional regard for that term and for the imagery surrounding it...mankind looked at the principles surrounding what the Temple of Set espouses today in an imperfect but gut way for many centuries using the imagery of the Devil. Setians enjoy the sinister image, the colorful atmosphere of traditions of black magic. We like spookiness.[104]

These new satanists-cum-setians believe that 'the worship of Set is the worship of individualism'. Aquino believes that the individual should not allow himself to be absorbed back into the universal whole, but rather should fight for an ongoing separate existence. His consciousness should strive 'to evolve towards its own divinity through a deliberate exercise of the intelligence and will'. This glorification of self he called 'becoming', or 'coming into being'. He called this progress to personal divinity 'Xeper' (pronounced 'Kheffer') after the Egyptian hieroglyphic for 'to become'.

Dr Aquino has spent the last few years wondering what he was actually to become, following extensive FBI investigations regarding himself in particular and satanism in general.

On 14th August 1987, the San Francisco Police Department staged a raid on the Russian Hill home of Aquino and his wife,

Lilith. The raid followed allegations that Aquino's home had been the scene of a brutal child rape of a four-year-old girl. The principal suspect in the child molestation, a Baptist minister named Gary Hambright, was indicted on charges that he committed 'lewd and lascivious acts' with six boys and four girls ranging in age from three to seven years. One of the children identified Aquino as an abuser. Aquino, however, denied ever having met the child and accused the child's father, an assistant chaplain for the army, of trumping up the allegations in a Christian vendetta. Aquino and his wife were never indicted in the incident. Dr Aquino claimed that he had been in Washington DC at the time, enrolled in a year-long course at the National Defense University.

On a number of occasions, Aquino has asked for the courts to remove his name from the original court martial charge, but this has been denied each time because his alibi was not sufficient. It appears that despite Aquino's absence from the San Francisco Bay area, he had kept on his Russian Hill residence, and made frequent return trips.

At the height of the satanic ritual abuse controversy in England in 1991, I was co-operating with ITV's *The Cook Report* in an attempt to encourage authorities to hold a public enquiry into issues involved. Roger Cook managed to bring Michael and Lilith Aquino over to this country to answer questions on ritual abuse. They took the opportunity to formally recognise in ritual their British Magister David Austen, whom I later questioned in an attempt to understand the British side of Set.

Our meeting took place in the room next to his black-lined temple in his Lewisham flat which he shares with Richard, his gay partner. This homosexual reference is not meant as a snipe at Mr Austen, for he is in fact quite open about his sexuality. One of the subjects we used to break the ice was the hunt for London's serial gay killer, some of whose victims were from Austen's neighbourhood.

I then launched into a series of questions, beginning with numbers.

Me: How many belong to the British Temple?

Austen: We've gone for quality rather than quantity, and we'll have forty by the end of this week. If we had gone for quantity we would be upward of 300 members now...we get all sorts wanting to sell their souls to the devil...those wanting to get into orgies. We even had a woman...asking if she could be our next sacrifice.

Me: What happened to her?

Austen: She ended up at—[Austen mentioned a satanist and her northern group known to the author]. It has a bit of a bad name...this lady went up there, and she was abused; she was strapped to a step-ladder and assaulted...whipped and beaten...and it was pretty hair-raising to hear it [the dots in this quotation represent not abbreviations but activities of a pornographic nature]. We had a chap of seventeen contact us and we told him to come back when he was eighteen. But he ended up going to this group. It's a group that has people up [to the north] for whippings and orgies and that sort of thing.

Me: What do you believe about Set?

Austen: By the will, an individual magician can survive after death...as an energy existence; the *me* that's talking to you now. Set is symbolic of that. To the Egyptians, by the twentieth dynasty he was the bad boy of the gods; he had chopped his brother up to get rid of him...he was painted in the worst colours possible—white with red hair...hideous to the Egyptians! He was also supposed to be the god of homosexual rape. We use Set as a pointer, as a starting point.

Me: You obviously believe that there is no God. Where do you think the universe has come from?

Austen: Well, we don't really worry where it's come from. It's there. We believe that it's a natural phenomenon. We do believe that at some time Set has intervened in human development to mutate the human mind into what it is. We believe that he still intervenes, as when he sets apart his priests today...he did this with me.

Me: So Set is a being?

Austen: He's an entity, a psyche, a force. We don't worship it [sic]; we work, or walk, with him [sic] as a friend. We just see him as the next stage on for us. As he is now, we shall be, and as we are, he once was [a quote lifted straight out of Mormonism, where David Austen's beliefs and loyalties once lay].

Me: Does the Black Mass feature in your worship?

Austen: I had an Anglican upbringing and we both know that we don't quite see the bread as the body of Christ, and therefore, for me, a Black Mass does absolutely nothing. To an ex-Catholic, oh, they wax lyrical.

Me: What about sacrifices?

Austen: A sacrifice has to be willing...but there are other magical ways of achieving what we want...we consider ourselves above bestial acts. We don't consider blood to be the life force needed to power our rituals.

Me: How would you power your magic then?

Austen: Whatever you use is only a means to an end. You could talk of a curse...focusing your psychic energies on somebody...and there are lots of ways of doing it. It may appeal to one to do it with a wax doll, or another satanist would do it with a picture. You don't have to spill blood.

Me: What would you use your magic on?

Austen: Just recently, for instance, one of our adepts died— just twenty-eight he was—and we knew he wanted a temple funeral...Obviously, his family had a normal service, but we had our own necromantic rite afterwards [necromancy is relating to, or recalling, a dead body's spirit]. That was a means of communion; of having his presence there.

Me: You talk about remaining an individual and eventually evolving into your own personal god. Do you all end up as lots of little individual gods then?

Austen: We're going to be ongoing intellects, maybe have influences on some other life force or civilisation...We believe in the ongoing continuance of the individual intellect. How that develops post-mortem, not having been there, I can't really say.

Me: What I'm trying to understand is this: you're basing your life on Set. This is actually a life-and-death issue, because if you're right, I as a Christian minister am wrong. But if I'm right, you're wrong and there's hell to pay. You must obviously have good, strong reasons for basing your life on this. So what are the pillars, the unshakable pillars, on which you rest?

Austen: I don't like to use the word 'force', but there is that motivating force that you suddenly become aware of, and you then search to understand what it is. This motivating force we recognise as Set. We use that force in our magical workings...call on it...is present with us...and is a friend.

Me: But what is the evidence to show that your way is the right way?

Austen: Oh, I wouldn't say it's the right way; it won't be the right way for you. It's right for me. It's my personal initiatory experience. But at the end of the day it wouldn't be right for somebody else.

Me: So at the end, it's your experience and you just feel this is right!

Austen: Well, it's basically what does it for you. It's probably the worst word to use, but it's my spiritual home. It's where I'm happy. It's where I'm content. Here I am.

Such a quote has echoes in every conversation I have ever had with occultists, be they satanists, witches, psychics, New Age travellers or whoever. They swim in a sea of feelings in an ocean of doubt. They illustrate more vividly than most the dark, quiet revolution which is moving society away from using brains and reason to feelings and intuition.

A great writer of the past once pointed to where man should anchor his life, and then added: 'Then we will no longer be infants, tossed back and forth by the waves, and blown here and there by every wind of teaching and by the cunning and craftiness of men in their deceitful scheming' (St Paul writing to the Ephesians who had their own occult problems—chapter 4, verse 14). As to the anchor for man's life, we come to that later, in the chapter dealing with answers to your questions.

As we leave the public way of satanism to penetrate the hidden paths of Britain's darker magic, we will find that the search by feelings is even more dominant.

10

Into the Shadows

> Like Faust, we have made our pact with the mighty powers of darkness. No boundary can halt our quest for dominion. We are a Satanic Leadership School, imparting black magical power that shall enable our elite to rise as future leaders in every field.[105]

The number of satanists in Britain today is anybody's guess.

This is the worst possible answer for a researcher anxious for truth, but it is better than guessing. I am convinced that not even the satanists themselves know, for most covens, temples and lodges are lost in the shadows of an occult world where trust and sharing are in short supply.

The satanic numbers game ranges between two extremes. On the one hand are those who laugh off satanism as a myth, while on the other, there is one outlandish claim made by a BBC *Panorama* interviewee that an unbelievable 10% of the population were satanists.[106] The only time this was possibly ever true of any Western nation was in pre-Revolution France, and then it was probably only 10% of the aristocracy. More credible guesstimates of 'about 10,000' were offered by BBC and ITV news programmes at the height of the satanic child abuse controversy, and it was this figure that Marc Europe used in its statistical compilations for its *UK Christian Handbook*. The latest 1994 edition entry, however, was reduced to 1,000 satanists (retaining the 10,000 figure in brackets) on the basis that only 10% of any religious group are committed.[107]

A total of 10,000 was also extrapolated from *The Occult Census*,[108] but when I queried this figure with organiser Chris Bray at his Sorcerer's Apprentice premises, he suggested that this was probably too high. He explained that only 300 of his 60,000 mail-order clients could be classified as satanists. Of course, the Sorcerer's Apprentice is only one of a dozen or so large occult enterprises in Britain, and there are many additional small one-man businesses dotted about the nation's high streets and back streets. Mr Bray's 300 has to be multiplied accordingly.

The real numbers lie hidden somewhere in the shadows of this chapter which investigates the less-than-public face of satanism, the full features of which not even the satanists themselves have gazed upon. The groups mentioned here represent only the pinnacle of a largely-hidden iceberg, and for one simple reason: satanism is becoming increasingly the path of the solitary occultist, practising his lonely black art in some do-it-yourself temple in the corner of a bedroom, or some dusty dedicated cellar. He is seeking power for himself and is not too bothered about anybody else.

Church of Satan leader Anton LaVey supports this point in his latest book *The Devil's Notebook*,[109] claiming that his own theories and aspirations are now being used by ordinary men and women in their own private lives. In an *Observer* newspaper interview he said that this represented a new wave of satanism which involved a 'growing misanthropy and desire for isolation'. His book advocates the creation of 'artificial human companions' to facilitate 'politically correct slavery' and the creation of 'total environments': adult Disneylands where a person can surround himself with a fantasy world of his own choice.[110]

We may not be able to track down Satan's lone suburban her-mits, but some detective work has unearthed the following groups.

Orthodox Temple of the Prince

This group practises Benelism ('non-malefic satanism') and it has emerged from the shadows only on rare occasions during its history. The last time it did so—rather rashly in the limelight of a television studio—was in the form of high priest Ramon, who promptly found himself undergoing trial by television and, subsequently, by the tabloids.

He was inevitably found guilty because the media—acting as both judge and jury in the satanic abuse storm at the time—were seriously hunting for ritual abuse culprits. To be a satanist of any description at that time and in that climate was to be automatically condemned.

Ramon (real name Dr Raymond Bogart) did have the chance to defend himself during the television programme concerned, ITV's *The Time and the Place*. When reporter John Merry suddenly denounced him on air as a satanist with a conviction as a child sex offender, programme presenter Mike Scott allowed time for the accused to reply. However, a flustered Ramon seemed to make matters worse for himself as he struggled, and failed, to find the correct 'sound bites' for his defence.

I sat near him during the exposé and his subsequent half-hearted defence, and felt a strange sympathy towards him. I was certainly on the programme to speak against satanism, including Ramon and his beliefs, but it was another thing to be suddenly involved in what fell woefully short of British justice. It reminded me of my own 'trials by television' when I was hopelessly outnumbered by occult practitioners on BBC's *Kil-roy* and Granada Television's *Up Front*. Trials are never pleasant, but trials by television can be horrific.

Later, at the invitation of an occult magazine, Dr Bogart, who lives near my parish in Lancashire, was able to put forward a more reasoned account:

> The T.V. programme...was definitely set up to give a very biased view of our religion. Nothing we do has the remotest connection with child sacrifices and sex orgies. About my past, I was falsely accused of illegal sex with a 15-year-old girl, and I have spent the last 20 or so years trying to erase this from my life. I have since gained a degree in psychology and theology and am now well respected in my field, both locally and throughout the country. Without appearing conceited I could show you letters of thanks from people whom I have helped, and if it was not for these letters of support, I don't know how I would have survived the last few weeks since the T.V. programme.[111]

Dr Bogart failed to tell the magazine readers that he had served a four-year prison sentence for the offence and that he had also practised privately as a child psychologist. However, that stated, I would not wish on anybody the television and tabloid treatment that he received.

Dr Bogart, who now tells me that he no longer leads the Orthodox Temple of the Prince, once confided in me that he had seventeen lodges operating between Manchester and Newcastle. His beliefs are 'taken from very early translated and transliterated scriptures dated about 5,000 B.C.E. [before Common Era] originating from the Sumerian civilisation. The scriptures describe the beginning of pure Benelism [non-malefic satanism].[112]

The belief system is detailed in the temple's 'Brief Explanatory Letter to Enquires': 'Orthodox BENELism is the belief in BENEL as The SON OF GOD, through whom we invoke power from God to bring to successful conclusions the rituals which we perform, and as the successes of our rituals are so extremely high, we know that the beliefs we have, and the rituals we do, are more correct than any other beliefs...'[113]

Christianity is considered wrong, and Jesus Christ the

usurper of Benel's position. The letter explains that because the order's god is so supreme and unapproachable, supplications need to go through his son Benel. It continues:

> We believe in ASHTAROTH the Queen of Heaven...who ensures the welfare of our families...These then are the Triarchy of the ancients we believe in...Our religion, originating as it did some 10,000 years ago...is the University of Life, for it teaches us to understand ourselves and others. As occultists we study the Mysteries of Life and the meaning of love...and best of all, how to help and cure the sick in mind and body.
>
> When it is absolutely necessary, we practise retribution against malicious and evil people, but only when we are forced to do so...The Sabbat meetings are (near enough) every four weeks and there are six Grand Sabbats a year. We meet in ordinary clothes, but at rituals we wear our robes.
>
> Our religion doesn't build great monoliths, or amass great wealth. Our religion is about people...Our teachings are numerous and expansive...On the occult side we have some 300 subjects... including Tarot, Astrology...Candle and Incense Magic...how to deal with hauntings and poltergeists...We bless those who are good, and where necessary we curse those who are continually and intentionally evil.

The letter moves on to stress what the temple is not about: 'WE DO NOT indulge in human sacrifice or vampirism. We do not practise any perverse or anti-Christian rituals, nor do we curse people for not following our beliefs. There are NO orgies of Sex, Drink or Drugs...All-Male or All-Female Circles are not allowed. Circle members do not practise in the nude.'

The letter makes one claim that, even in normal circumstances, would be difficult to believe: 'There is no dissent amongst our people, and jealousy is unknown.' The circumstances surrounding my first dealings with those coming out of the Orthodox Temple of the Prince make it hard to accept this claim.

A family telephoned one Saturday evening asking for help to extricate themselves from one of the temple's groups. They said that the main priest of their particular group had insisted on performing the Act of Unity on the altar with their fourteen-year-old daughter. The mother had pointed out that her daughter was under the legal age for sexual intercourse, but the high priest had explained that the order had its own calendar, and according to this, she was nineteen.

The father of the family was not so much concerned about his daughter, but rather the Acts of Unity he himself had been ordered to perform on the temple's Altar of Initiation.

'It wasn't fair,' he complained. 'The main priest got all the good-looking ones while I was left with the old fat ones.' The father's real purpose in allowing me to visit the family was not so much to get help, but to recoup the £40 he had spent on his copy of the temple's scriptures by selling them to me. When I refused to buy them, he lost interest. His daughter summed up the emotions of herself and her mother: 'We were supposed to follow our scriptures,' she explained, 'but all he [the main priest] did was to change them or make up extra things to suit what he wanted to do. There's no way he's going to do what he wants to with me on his altar!'

Shortly after Dr Bogart told me he was no longer involved with the order, two freelance female reporters commissioned by the *News of the World* to infiltrate satanic groups visited the doctor's home, suitably wired for sound. The reporters were specially chosen because they could pass for young girls.

Tracy, Schaverien and Kathy Evans reported that Dr Bogart had warned, 'You'll have to keep quiet. This can be our secret as you are only fifteen and shouldn't be doing this. You must be prepared to do things you might not want to... When you join a coven in my oreer you have to have sex with the High Priest... Sex is very important to us. It creates energy to make spells work. But you'll have to get used to strangers touching you.'[114]

Temple of Olympus (also known as Ordo Astrum Serpentis)

Proclaiming 'Love * Beauty * Joy * Truth—The time has come', this group advertised itself as 'a manifestation of the olympic current', and members were told:

> Truth is knowledge, not belief
> Truth is certainty, not faith
> Truth is attained by the love, beauty and joy in
>   the worship & mysteries of the Goddesses and Gods
>   of Olympus.
> Choose Knowledge
> Choose Certainty.[115]

It turned out to be anything but the truth for those who answered the advertisements. They found themselves in an occult temple in a terraced house in Limes Road, Croydon, in the midst of black magic rituals involving animal sacrifice and bizarre sexual acts.

The credit for the public exposé of this group goes to Sean Manchester and the Holy Grail, a London-based ministry to those in the cults and the occult. Sean discovered the group's secrets and later published them in a privately-printed booklet *From Satan to Christ*. He wrote that coven leaders recruited young people through adverts placed in occult bookshops and magazines. He added, in a leaflet accompanying his book:

In the past they have used Wicca or witchcraft as an introduction and training period for members who seldom realise they have joined a satanic group. The teachings of Aleister Crowley and his anti-Christian religion, Thelema, are also quickly introduced. After initiation, however, the sinister secrets of the coven soon reveal themselves and members regularly engage in black masses where indecency, animal cruelty and sacrilege take place. Female coven members are encouraged to enter prostitution...All members are made to decapitate a live animal during rituals.

Sean's revelations were picked up by Jackie McKeown, then a reporter with the *Croydon Advertiser*, who asked the coven leader, computer expert Mark Pastellopoulos, what was happening. He explained: 'What we were interested in was bringing back some of the beauty and splendour of classical religion. We had rituals in which we tried to celebrate nature, but the whole thing got out of hand.'[116]

Mr Pastellopoulos then confirmed that animals had been sacrificed during rituals, sex rites had taken place in the temple and at least one member of his group was involved in prostitution. He added, 'I surmise that if there were others, she introduced them to it. I never knew anything about it.'

Mr Pastellopoulos told the reporter that the group had disbanded, even though the altar was still in his home.

A knowledgeable London witch told me at the time of writing this chapter that a temple similar to the above was still in existence in the Croydon part of London, though she said the leadership was not known.

'It's very much undercover,' she added. 'A really nasty bit of work, I understand.'

Chaos magic

Including this group in a chapter on satanism will be about as welcome to Chaos magicians as associating the British Conservative Party with the old communists. The chao-ist considers him/herself to be on an altogether different intellectual plane; far superior to 'mere inadequate satanists', as one described it.

But the truth sometimes hurts, and the truth in this case is that there are distinct parallels between the two. Both satanists and chao-ists find themselves borrowing freely from each other.

Chaos magic is a reaction against all previous authority, tradition and leadership in the world and in the occult. Its only law is: 'Do whatever you like; all things are permissible.' The chaoist is interested only in that which works, and he will draw on all paths of the occult, including the various strands of satanism, to fulfil his magical needs.

Chaos magicians laugh at the idea of a Satan figure, but its philosophies and practices can be traced back to the experiments and explorations of arch-satanist Aleister Crowley, and the Golden Dawn, 'with all the crud cut out'.[117] Satanists in the Order of the Nine Angles readily embrace Chaos magic, and according to one of the ONA's *Fenrir* magazines the essence of satanism is chaos.[118] The chao-ist would also state that his magic is 'the culmination of all other systems', including satanism.[119] The ONA also promotes relationships with Chaos by advertising its journal *Chaos International*. As with satanism, there are no morals; no right and wrong beyond that which the individual chooses for him/herself. Both are about anarchy—individuals ruling themselves with few holds barred.

Society of the Dark Lily

This is 'the Reality of the Left Hand Path', according to the society's journal, *Dark Lily*. It likes to think of itself as the British voice of Anton LaVey's Church of Satan, and everything that has been written about the American Church of Satan applies also to Dark Lily. Everything, that is, except openness.

Enquirers can obtain a society magazine easily, and even a letter of thanks with the duplicated signature, 'Magda' (Magdalene Graham, Dark Lily's high priestess), on receipt of a £4 annual subscription. However, sending letters requesting interviews to the London contact box number seems as effective as putting your mail in the dustbin. Nobody answers!

Perhaps Magda has given up trying to communicate

satanism to non-satanists because she considers that the words and ideas employed to describe her religion are 'always derogatory or demeaning'. This is the view of the anonymous leader writer in *Dark Lily* (issue 15), who blames this on the nation's Christian culture. The writer argues that the dominant culture always protects itself by colouring its language against the minorities it fears.

The writer is, of course, quite right, as the first Christians knew to their cost in places like Antioch. When the citizens of the dominant pagan culture first coined the name 'Christian' it was done so in a 'derogatory and demeaning' way (Acts 11:26). However, the Christians answered this by turning the world and its language upside down with teachings and practices that transformed Christianity from a swear-word into a by-word for all that was good.

The *Dark Lily* leader writer criticises the Christian 'cultural supremacism', implying it should stand aside and let satanism be heard.

Werewolf Order

'We are the shocktroops of a youth uprising against Judeo-Christian tyranny: the focus of a return to the ancient pagan/satanic tradition that is the birthright of Western European men and women.' So begins an article in *NOX, the occult magazine of the Abyss*, explaining that the order exists 'to unleash the Beast in Man'.[120]

This is one of the rare satanic groups who actually talk in terms of signing a pact with the devil. The article explains: 'Like Faust, we have made our pact with the mighty powers of darkness. No boundary can halt our quest for dominion. We are a Satanic Leadership School, imparting black magical power that shall enable our elite to rise as future leaders in every field.'

The order works on the principle that the nineties will be an inversion of the sixties. Soft permissiveness will become the hard, brutal instilling of the satanic way. It boasts of bringing chaos, out of which will rise a 'new aesthetic and law'. Its members talk of unleashing the power of satanic youth and 'woe to the Judeo-Christian death cult and its lackeys!'.

The Werewolf Order is based in Los Angeles, California, and has a significant following in Britain due to advertising and 'public relations' within occult literature. It calls itself an 'elite sodality [sic] of black magicians who are creating a new world order based on satanic principles'. Its recruitment slogans claim: 'No longer can the beast in man be restrained by the leash of Judeo-Christian sheep morality. The wolfpack has gathered, summoned by the Call of the Wild. Rise!'

The order's spokesman is Nikolas Schreck, frontman of the 'gothic' band Radio Werewolf, a musical offshoot from the main order. Schreck is editor of the definitive book on jailed satanist Charles Manson, entitled *The Manson File* (Amok Press). He believes that the Werewolf Order is in the frontline of a 'demonic revolution'.

Ordo Templi Orientis (OTO)

The Order of Eastern Templars, to use its English title, has several hundred thousand members and hundreds of lodges in dozens of countries. That is about as precise as outsiders can be as they try to distinguish the shadowy features of this well-hidden facet of satanism and the occult. Other investigators have included the FBI in the States and similar law enforcement agencies around the world.

Few in the OTO would actually admit the existence of Satan, let alone pay tribute to him, but the organisation has many things in common with satanism. As we have already noted in Chapter 4, a major part of the OTO was taken over by Aleister Crowley in the twenties and was fashioned according to his satanic beliefs. Crowley used the name 'Baphomet', the satanic goat figure, because this idol had been worshipped by the original Knights Templars.

Today, a large part of the organisation is known as the Caliphate OTO, with a caliph chosen by senior order members. Its members rise in a system of degrees, and the higher the degree attained the greater the commitment to the order and Thelema—the law of the will. This law is the essence of selfish satanism claiming, 'Every man and woman is a star,' and, 'Do what thou wilt shall be the whole of the law.' The higher degrees (8, 9 and 11) are based on sexual magic—autosexual, heterosexual and homosexual.

Part of the OTO ritual is the Crowley-composed Gnostic Mass which, according to Caliphate OTO leader Gerald Suster, is a rite which 'centres around a priestess who is exalted upon an altar. She says little, yet in practice is the most important of the celebrants, since it is she who brings the power through.'[121]

This mass also reveals a link between pagans, witches, the OTO and satanists. Suster adds: 'Though the Mass may seem a bit alien to many pagans, it should be remembered that sections have been incorporated into the Great Rite, the third and highest Wiccan Initiation.'

Suster says that the present OTO is a continuation of Crowley's OTO, adding:

In his time and since, parts of the order have split off and some continue to use the title OTO. Some of these offshoots do useful work...The Order is headed by a Caliph...the Caliph charters the heads of national and local bodies, the mistress or master of which is responsible for its actions. This authority extends to order business and no further. The activities of the groups vary greatly, both in this country and internationally. These activities include study groups, group ritual work, and Gnostic Masses, meetings and parties.

Temple Ov Psychick Youth (TOPY):

TOPY's present leadership reluctantly admits that 'some members' did lean towards satanism 'at one particular time', but it now insists that this no longer applies. Some members went down the path travelled by the likes of satanist Charles Manson, 'but only to understand them and to see how they occurred'. TOPY, its leadership promises, has now matured into a respectable and intellectual esoteric organisation.

These assurances come from Paul Cecil, the spokesman for the international temple, which in 1982 grew out of, and alongside, rock group Psychic TV, headed by Genesis P-Orridge.

P-Orridge, at one time assistant editor of *Occulture*, TOPY's magazine, was not only heavily into the occult, but also sado-masochism, including body-piercing, according to sixteen-pages of full-frontal photographs and a magazine interview.[122] However, I was assured by Paul Cecil that Genesis P-Orridge and his fully co-operative partner and wife, Paula, had ceased to be connected with TOPY and now lived in America.

Had Mr P-Orridge become an embarrassment to the temple? Was that why they parted company?

'No, there was never any rift in that sense,' Paul Cecil explained. 'He [P-Orridge] went through a phase in his life when he wanted to explore a particular way of doing things. He had done that. He probably lost interest in the group and wanted to move on.'

Mr Cecil assured me that the membership of TOPY had undergone a complete change in recent years. There had been several hundred associated with the temple over the years, but a new membership had now taken it into other areas. There were still those interested in shamanism, the occult and magic, but many more pursuing interests in the media, sciences, literature and psychology.

'The basic essence of TOPY,' assured Mr Cecil, 'is that

people are free to explore in whatever areas they choose. There's no central dogma; no central belief structure.'

The Vampire Society

Carole Bohanan founded this group in the late eighties and, like the Temple of Olympus, it is based in the Croydon area. Ms Bohanan and her colleagues get annoyed when people associate them with black magic or satanism.

'Our members are all ages and range from students to accountants. We get occasional approaches from people who are into black magic, but we tell them we're just not like that,' Ms Bohanan told the *News of the World*.[123]

Another Vampyre Society leader Pandora Corey said on the *South Bank Show*: 'It makes me very angry that people think that just because you dress in black or wear a bat or something, that they think you are interested in Satan and the occult. It's not true at all.'[124]

Yet the membership of the society has a definite satanic leaning. David Austen of the Temple of Set is a leading member, and the *Velvet Vampyre*, a society publication, abounds with membership requests that certainly compromise the society, if nothing else. Members clearly advertise for information on satanic leaders of the past, and on associated satanic and witchcraft rites like necromancy.[125]

Ganymede

This small group appears to have been teetering on the brink of extinction in recent years since several other occult publications banned its promotional advertisements because of its open support for illegal paedophilia. However, Ganymede continues to operate out of its Wiltshire base at a reduced and more secret level than before. It goes on advocating worship of the

'Lord of Dark Lusts' and describes itself as 'an open forum for Gay and Bi-sexual initiates involved with the esoteric sciences'.[126]

The real problem

As I have already indicated, for every group I have uncovered, there is evidence that there are a dozen more.

There is the Acid House Party connection. 'A nightmare in Hell' promised one underground, professionally-produced ticket to an acid freakout in Lancashire. It was run by Hell Rave Promotions, and halfway through the night a goat was ceremonially slaughtered, cooked and later served up in a dawn breakfast soup. They promised 'a hurricane of laser and sound to end the world—13 demented hours for you to panic and scream' and it featured satanic numbers from heavy metal favourites.

There are also the chapters of Hell's Angels and Satan's Slaves. Those whom I have caught up with in lay-bys or wherever, simply grunt that they know nothing of satanism and just want to be left alone to roar through the countryside. But listening to many of their right-wing views makes me suspect that there is more than idyllic rural thoughts beneath the crash helmets covered with swastikas and black-magic symbols.

The modern neo-Nazi link

During my research, a strong connection emerged between satanism and the extreme right-wing political parties, though not a hint of this surfaced in the press coverage of the sensational Isle of Dogs by-election victory of British National Party candidate Derek Beacon in September 1993.

The BNP victory was variously attributed to a local tradition of extreme right-wing support dating back to Mosley, disillusionment with mainstream parties in one of Britain's most deprived inner-city areas, the insularity of the white community, and even an allegedly racist campaign by the Liberal Democrats.

But one thing is certain, many of the satanists whom I have interviewed spoke of their involvement with right-wing politics.

A founding member of the Dark Lily was a leading member of the British Movement, while some of the present members spice up their sado-masochistic leanings with what is termed 'theatrical Nazism'—parading and cavorting about in the regalia of the Third Reich. Various members of the Order of Nine Angles also belong to extreme right-wing groups. Members of other satanist groups are members of the British National Party, mainly because the BNP is 'very Odinistic, following the Nordic blond-hair-blue-eyes Thunder God'. A leader of another British satanist group acknowledged that he had infiltrated to the very top of the National Front in its hey day, while others, like Christos of the ONA, claimed to use the extreme right wing for their own purposes. Remember this statement in Chapter 8 when he was speaking about satanists wanting a 'forward-looking society...one which is similar to the Vikings'? This is what Christos added: '...National Socialism is often used by satanists because that is really one of only a few political forms which enshrine that idea. We don't necessarily believe in those right-wing Nazi groups, but we do think they can be used to bring about change and a new order.'

And quite a change the neo-Nazi by-election victory proved to be.

Of course it was a freak event, and of course it couldn't ever happen again in England, stressed the political commentators. However, many exultant BNP supporters would beg to differ.

'We are on the threshold of history,' cried one at the victory celebration. 'Nothing can stop us now.'

Britain's satanists most certainly will not be applying the brakes. Many of them will be pushing hard from within right-wing politics to bring radical change.

With many satanic groups, only infiltration can secure first-hand information, but joining them means progressively practising their degrees and rituals. These groups give nothing until they have received everything. They include:

The Church of Satanic Liberation – led by a Paul Douglas Valentine, based in New Haven, Connecticut, which advertises in England.

Daughters of Baphomet—an offshoot from the Order of Nine Angles, which operates in the West Midlands and refuses to communicate with any who are not members.

ONA (the old order). This is more a description than the official name of this satanic group. All that is known by outsiders is that it is a homosexual temple made up of the "old guard" members of the Order of Nine Angles.

Order of the Left-Hand Path—a satanic group using hermetic magic which is based in New Zealand, but has a following in England.

The Feminine Satanic Witch—an embarrassment to both satanists and witches who both swear that each has nothing to do with the other. The satanic witches' views are published in their group's voice *The Scroll*.

Unnamed, often unknown groups—covens, temples or lodges spring up for a time, satisfy their desires and then die away. One trying to start up at the time of writing is in Felixstowe and is advertising for members under the name of P. Meister. Perhaps the most famous of these types of groups was headed up by Derry Mainwaring Knight who began his own satanic temple in London in the eighties, before being jailed for defrauding Christians out of a quarter of a million pounds.[127] This section of the satanic must include all the other individuals who have come before the crown courts of our land, some of whom are detailed in Chapters 2 and 3.

It is significant that none of the satanic individuals who have appeared before the courts have claimed to belong to the more

publicly-recognised satanic groups. Some were obviously acting on their own satanic initiative, but others were members of
some temple or group. Perhaps they belonged to groups similar
to those which are mentioned in the testimony of ritual abuse
victims. Beacon Foundation, which has counselled and helped
many of the victims, lists several groups in its booklet *The
Rehabilitation of Satanic Cult Members*.[128]

These are the groups, followed by quoted descriptions from
foundation director Maureen Davies:

Druidic satanism. 'This is old, international and appears to
be up and coming in this country. It is very violent.'

The Brotherhood. 'This is an international order operating in
the UK. It is very old, and many generational satanists [people
who have been brought up as satanists within the family] are
involved. It is very violent.'

Order of Dagon. 'This appears to be a generational satanic
order, involved in international criminal acts.'

Temple of Britannia. 'The elite British satanic order, dealing
with political issues. Many of its members have positions of
power in society.'

Sisters of Kali. 'This is the temple prostitute order for Britannia. They are involved in sadistic lesbianism, and other sexual
deviations.' Victims have spoken of this group targeting the
mentally handicapped and children.

The Cromlech Temple. 'Assigned to do the same as Sisters of
Kali...also a lesbian freemasonry society.'[129]

Temple of Ishtar. 'Run for generational satanists.'

The Black Snake. 'West Indian satanic order.' Also known as
La Coueuve Noir.

This Beacon Foundation list is not without its critics. For
example, Temple of Set leader David Austen wrote to me:
'Maureen Davies is spinning you a yarn with some of these
groups, or gotten her facts wrong...Druidic satanism would be
something of an anathema to the Druids and is absolutely

ridiculous...I love Maureen's continued fantasy about generational satanism. Satanism, of whatever division, requires that each initiate enter its path of their own free will.'

Jill, from the Midlands, would disagree with Mr Austen and suggest that he himself still has much to learn about some forms of satanism, especially the generational form she was initiated into by her 'great grandma' as a child—Druidic satanism!

Jill told me.

I experienced the blood rites, the power, domination and, most of all, the fear. The Druidic satanists I belonged to were not those oh-so-nice respectable types dancing about in their robes and spouting poetry. This is the dark side of Druidism, based on the sacred oak beliefs of Druidism. The groups I knew were called the Brotherhood of the Sacred Oak, the Brotherhood of the Dark Oak, or simply just Children of Danu.

It was cruel. You found yourself trapped in a vicious circle: first you hate it, then you begin to get used to it, and then you want it. There were all types of abuse going on—physical, sexual, emotional, psychological...there were threats of beating to ensure our silence; there was also the knowledge that others who did not obey were pushed to the point of suicide.

Throughout my childhood [she's now approaching thirty], I was still under the influence of the group, even after my great grandma died...When I was fifteen, I eventually plucked up courage to talk to my parents about it. I knew that my great grandma had tried to draw them in, but they had refused. When I asked them questions, they immediately rounded on me, told me to stay silent about it all, and especially never to talk about it outside the family.

Jill has been a member of a Midlands Baptist church for seven years at the time of writing, but is still struggling with her past. She was actually sent to the church to cause disruption, but found what she described as 'a church that actually practised what it preached' and which 'had a power that I couldn't break'.

Apart from the above satanic groups, others mentioned by research contacts include The Fraternity & Children of Lucifer, based around London's Regent's Park; Acadia in Watford; the Temple of Amoun in Bristol; Anglican Satanic Church, based in King's Lynn; The AntiChrist Society; Kna'anim, with connections with Arab terrorists; Septum Sathani; Monastica Parternalis, based around Lowndes Square, London; the Precise and True Temple of Isis, in Mayfair and Kilburn, and Adytum Trivia, in Bloomsbury, London.

I could find nobody who would openly talk about these groups beyond acknowledging their existence.

If the hidden satanists will not talk, the next best option is to listen to, and assess, what the victims say...

11

The Victims

It would seem to me that since children quite literally all over the world are independently disclosing very specific details of quite bizzare abuse—details they could not possibly have fantasised—either we have a massive international conspiracy of toddlers or else there's some form of intelligent adult organisation involved.[130]

Child therapist

There are several hundred victims of ritual abuse in Britain alone. This was the claim of one reputable author, Andrew Boyd, after spending a year interviewing professional carers across the nation.[131] He recorded a total of 900 victims, though he suggested that this figure could involve some duplication.

However, before we weigh the evidence of victims, we need to assess how reliable they are—not an easy task after five controversial years of claims and counter-claims between psychologists, psychiatrists, clergy, social workers and police in the wake of Rochdale and the Orkneys. It is not this book's brief to try and solve this Stygian problem, for this has been attempted extensively, and ably, elsewhere.[132] However, we do need to at least note the main pros and cons.

First the case against...

Not ritual abuse but...

'The nightmare that never was' blazed the *Daily Mail* across two pages of its edition on 25th April 1994, after getting a sneak preview of Professor La Fontaine's official report into the extent and nature of organised and ritual abuse. The sub-heading ran, 'Church groups blamed for spreading myths about Satan's children'. Journalists, police and an assortment of current affairs experts had all tried to explain away satanic ritual abuse as a myth before the professor's official effort. Their combined reasoning went as follows.

At first, it was assumed that paedophile rings had adopted weird satanic regalia and rituals to instil fear into their victims, and so make detection less likely.

Next, the mantle of blame came to rest on fundamentalist Christians, who, it was alleged, had deliberately 'demonised' satanists as child abusers or baby-eaters, so that society would back a crusade against the occult, and believe in the reality of a devil.

Social workers were then accused of being hoodwinked at abuse conferences attended or led by fundamentalist Christians, where they were allegedly inspired to return to their own patches to root out satanic ritual abuse.

Some of the lesser culprits for spreading the 'myth', it was stated, were the mentally ill or disturbed women who saw a fresh way of securing more attentive audiences.

Placed into this category especially were the alleged cases of False Memory Syndrome. These were women who were supposed to have recalled childhood traumas with the help of therapists who believed that their clients' problems were the result of some early-life abuse hidden in the subconscious. This has now become a highly-controversial area, with emotional outbursts in the high decibels, especially among those middle-aged or elderly parents who have suddenly found themselves accused of abusing their adult children. This has led to accused parents uniting together for support in the False Memory Syndrome Foundation and Adult Children Accusing Parents.

One of the more ingenious denials of ritual abuse proposed that some deep sociological fear within society had made women imagine ritual abuse. For instance, it was claimed that the alleged ritual abuse of children in American day-care centres was merely a myth created by a society scared of losing control of its children. Mothers felt that their children were increasingly being brought up in contractual relationships (in the centres) rather than in covenantal relationships (in the home). Mothers resented this loss, forced on them by the need to work, and therefore any hint of danger to their children was magnified out of all proportion—hence the ritual abuse cry![133]

Another sociologist has explained that far from being a reality, ritual abuse is merely memory traces inherited from our ancestral past.[134] This theory, based on the Carl Jung concept of the 'collective unconscious', suggests that stories of ritual abuse are actually 'recollections' dredged up from the events of previous stages in our evolution, or past lives as humans, or even animals.

Before reviewing the arguments for accepting ritual abuse as a reality, a few words about the above.

True, paedophiles could have changed their *modus operandi* to include the theatricals of satanism, but even so it would still be ritual abuse, at least as far as the children were concerned. True, Christians have helped lead ritual abuse conferences, but mainly because very few in society would listen to the children's cries. However, critics have to be somewhat detached from the real world to believe that experienced, case-hardened, sometimes cynical social workers could be hoodwinked by a handful of allegedly dotty Christians.

The False Memory Syndrome should certainly be taken seriously, and we do so later in this chapter. The possibility of haunting sociological fears of American mothers may be a possibility with some guilt-ridden mums, but the US courts did find sufficient evidence to send at least two dozen proven ritual abusers to prison.

The last reason for trying to dismiss ritual abuse—the recourse to past-life trace memories—reveals more about the unhappy, sometimes desperate, state of modern sociology and sociologists than the ritual abuse problem.

A case for believing

1. Humanity is more than capable of ritual abuse.

It seems rather obvious to state that man is capable of such evil, especially when we recall the experiments with, and the gassing of, millions of adults and children at the hands of the Nazis. It becomes even more obvious as we see daily on the TV that hundreds of thousands of children are being abused and killed in forty-odd war zones as I write. But it appears that there are still some who cherish the idea that modern Western man could not dream of such nastiness, despite the rocketing figures of domestic child abuse.

2. Child abuse, even child sacrifice, has happened many times throughout our history, whether it is modern Third World parents disposing of uneconomic female babies, or Herod's genocide, or the Old Testament sacrifice of children to Molech.[135]

3. Satanism has encouraged ritual abuse and even child sacrifice in the past, and continues to do so today, through the writings of Crowley and groups like the Order of Nine Angles.[136] Should we be too surprised if some modern satanists follow the inspiration of leading satanists?

4. The court cases outlined in Chapter 3 above present a strong case for the reality of ritual abuse. The evidence was not simply a concoction of old wives' tales, nor the meanderings of deranged imaginations.

It was real evidence of real events given through real tears.

5. Evidence of ritual abuse was often given freely and unexpectedly by children. It included knowledge way beyond their young years, which not even nasty videos could impart. One social worker and child therapist said: 'It would seem to me that since children quite literally all over the world are independently disclosing very specific details of quite bizzare abuse— details they could not possibly have fantasised—either we have a massive international conspiracy of toddlers or else there's some form of intelligent adult organisation involved.'[137]

6. Ritual abuse began to be accepted because of the credibility and consistency of the carers, including the NSPCC, Childwatch, the National Children's Home, The Children's Society, Reachout Trust, The Beacon Foundation and others.

In summary: satanism exists. Some forms of satanism advocate abuse of children, and even child sacrifice. There is mounting evidence of ritual abuse in the criminal and family courts of the land.

Does it not therefore seem reasonable, at the very least, to pay attention to at least some of what these 900 ritual abuse victims are saying?

It seemed more than reasonable to thirty-eight consultants, doctors, psychiatrists, psychologists, psychotherapists and social workers who united their professional experience to produce *Treating Survivors of Satanist Abuse*, under the editorship of Valerie Sinason, Consultant Child Psychotherapist at the Tavistock Clinic, St George's Hospital and the Anna Freud Centre, London.

Treating Survivors of Satanist Abuse 'records the process of survivors' treatment'. It also records honest 'fears and doubts of the therapists as they listen to detailed accounts of perversion and extreme cruelty'. It offers 'definitions of ritual abuse and analyses some of the reasons for societal disbelief'. It goes on to "examine the predicament of survivors who have experienced major trauma" only for them to be told by an unsympathetic world that they have imagined it all.[138]

The victims

One harrowing testimony after another could now be presented, but that would require more than the pages of this book, and then we would still have to evaluate them and construct an overall judgement. It is here that the extensive research work of university lecturer Patricia Anne Campbell Hughes can help us. This qualified psychologist has produced a scientific analysis of many ritual abuse testimonies with the help of seventy-seven professional and voluntary carers throughout the country.[139] A third were counsellors, a quarter were fellow psychologists or psychiatrists, and the rest were made up of police and probation officers, social service workers, clergy and foster parents. Each filled in an extensive questionnaire on each of the ritual abuse victims they treated.

All but two of the ritual abuse victims they helped were female, and the victims' ages ranged from thirteen to sixty-five years. Victims came from all walks of life, and included housewives, teachers, social workers, residential care workers, secretaries and nurses.

An astounding 84% of them were introduced to satanism through their families. A major part of the 'family religion' was sexual abuse, involving 97% of the victims. A fifth reported torture, 62% reported physical and emotional abuse, and 26% engaged in bestiality.

Four out of five victims said that they had been threatened by abusers to ensure their silence. Nearly all said that as a consequence they were afraid of punishment if they disobeyed. Half of the victims said they were rewarded for co-operation.

When it came to the satanic belief system, 81% of victims

reported that they had been indoctrinated into believing, in general terms, that the flesh and ego were there to be gratified, and that life was about the exercise of power over others. Most believed in some form of power transference—taking in somebody else's energy or having power taken away from them. Most thought this could be done through ingesting somebody else's blood or through pain or sexual activity. There was also a belief that on the death of a victim, the life power transferred to the sacrificial executioner.

Three-quarters had had involvement in initiation rituals at certain ages, and other rituals had taken place for most on Christian festivals or on their own birthdays.

Professional carers reported that as a result of the abuse, victims suffered psychological problems on a large scale. Four out of five victims suffered flashbacks, and nearly half were self-destructive and indulged in self-mutilation. More than three-quarters suffered psychological problems involving depression, anxiety, anger, sleep disturbance and dissociation.

Patricia Hughes reported: 'A substantial number of clients (42 per cent) claimed a belief that they were possessed by evil spirits. Some of the literature suggests that in order to work successfully with this client group, the spiritual dimension cannot be ignored (Friesen 1991).'[140]

In addition to research into victims' evidence, Patricia Hughes looked—as have we in this book—at the origins of satanism, modern expressions of it, together with ritual abuse cases and theory, and she came to a seven-point conclusion, which I summarise.

1. Interviewing techniques

Alleged ritual abuse cases like those in Rochdale and Nottingham showed that the children's evidence was not believed.

Patricia Hughes counters this by writing: 'La Fontaine states that children do not often make false accusations of sexual abuse. This view is upheld by Giarretto, who stated at an NSPCC conference in London in 1990 that after treating 10,000 children, he could count on one hand the number of false allegations.'[141]

Proposal: Interviews of alleged victims should be conducted and taped by trained therapists or police, and they should be child-focused.

2. *Repressed memory—real or false?*

Do 'repressed' memories exist in reality? Is it possible that a child who is abused can find the experience so distasteful that she locks it away in the subconscious only to have it emerge at a vulnerable time in adulthood? Or are 'repressed' memories simply false memories planted in the minds of clients by badly-trained therapists, or therapists out to prove a theory?

There is an emotional controversy raging about this not only between parents and their adult children, but also between competing scientific schools of thought. Patricia Hughes adds: 'Many adults are coming forward disclosing childhood sexual abuse. La Fontaine (1990) has suggested that these disclosures may be the product of their willingness to talk and being at a distance from the event enables them to do so. The distance from the event could be one reason why people come forward in their adult lives with memories of childhood abuse.'

Proposal: The Scientific community should work together in researching into 'repressed memory' and 'False Memory Syndrome' instead of forming opposing organisations.

3. *The church*

Two-thirds of professional carers felt that the church was in need of further education on ritual abuse.

Patricia Hughes commended the Church of Scotland and the Council of Churches in Britain and Ireland for accepting the reality of child abuse and drawing up guidelines for dealing with survivors, but there was little education happening at grass-roots level. More in the church needed to note the 'increasing number of young people joining new religious movements and cults' and satanism.

There was also concern about clergy being too eager to perform exorcisms on those suffering from dissociative states. This was not necessarily demon possession.

Proposal: All clergy and trainee clergy should be educated about ritual abuse and dissociative disorders, and the church should be prepared to work with other disciplines, set up a network of information, educate the parishes and establish 'spiritual advisers' on the paranormal.

4. The police

The research showed that 58% of carers believed that the police were ill-equipped to deal with ritual abuse.

Some police forces have expressed a need for education into the belief system of satanism [reported Patricia Hughes], but sadly, some forces are not willing to accept the possible reality of its existence. Alleged survivors are disbelieved and dismissed as being mentally ill, or of fabricating tales.

Many police officers do not understand that a person who has been severely traumatised may not be able to give accounts of incidents and that it will take time and patience to obtain evidence.

Proposal: There should be training at all levels of the police force regarding satanism, and in particular about dissociation, post-traumatic stress syndrome and the role of female perpetrators.

5. Social services

Proposal: All levels should receive suitable training on ritual abuse. They should also receive specialised skills training in interviewing children, and be given help with the management of undisciplined feelings, all of which would help to avoid future mistakes.

6. Mental health

It appears that the human brain has many 'tricks' to help it cope with great trauma like prolonged ritual abuse in childhood. One is to block off the experiences completely and so repress the memory. Another is to dissociate and drift off into an alternative reality until the hurt goes away. But some victims have coped with trauma by developing another personality—an escape persona which can be assumed while trauma is at its worst. This apparently can become so ingrained that the personality is split into two or more independent parts (or persons).

Nearly a third of ritual abuse victims had been diagnosed at one time or another as suffering from Multiple Personality Disorder, 'and Frieson (1991) claims that as many as 97% of patients diagnosed as Multiple Personality Disorder have suffered serious abuse as children'.

More than half the carers who returned questionnaires thought that mental health workers were not sufficiently educated on the effects of ritual abuse.

Proposal: Mental health workers should receive training at all levels, with particular attention to the diagnosis and treatment of Multiple Personality Disorder, the management of addictive/compulsive behaviours, while at the same time receiving specialised supervision. A professional network should also be set up for support and exchange of ideas.

7. *The community*

Most carers believed that many of their clients' problems related directly to lack of support facilities within the community.

Proposal: Community based 'safe houses' and short-term care should be provided, plus a twenty-four-hour helpline staffed by those who understand problems related to ritual abuse.

Patricia Hughes stated as she concluded her proposals:

> The findings of this research and other unpublished research strongly suggest that there is a problem which needs to be addressed. It is an issue that simply cannot be tackled by any one individual or agency in isolation. What is needed in order to address the issue of satanic ritual abuse is a multi-disciplinary approach.
>
> According to the various reports on past cases, the starting point has been one of co-operation between the different agencies, but for one reason or another the system has broken down.

One possible reason for the breakdown, she explained, was that each discipline had a different task. The police needed evidence which was beyond reasonable doubt to secure conviction, while social services needed only reasonable doubt to remove the children from a suspect environment. It is therefore not unreasonable to find a conflict of interests.

There was another conflict of interest on the caring side. One group of professionals was primarily interested in the victim, while another group seemed to be set on discovering the truth about the abuse.

'Strictly from a counselling viewpoint,' concluded Patricia Hughes, we should be accepting the client's subjective reality and facilitating the journey of self-discovery, instead of trying to prove or disprove their statements...

To return to the proposal that a multi-disciplinary approach is needed...these should be represented by Social Services, police, the church, mental health, counsellors and voluntary agencies all working together...

Each agency needs to respect and understand the remit of the other agencies. Each agency must be willing to co-operate fully with the other agencies, and operate only within their own remit. Finally, the team must not lose sight of the fact that priority must be with the victim.[142]

PART TWO

Some Solutions

12
Your Questions Answered

Epistle writer Paul was a great 'therefore' man. Having set out a problem with clarity, he would often use this word to pivot attention towards the consequent solution or advice.

This is our 'therefore' moment. Bearing in mind all that has gone before, what do we do about it?

The secular book might stop here, but we have a 'therefore' God who hates to abandon his people in the face of problems. He produced the original 'how to...' book, enabling us to focus on the practical steps to be taken when spiritual issues go wrong.

The following is not so much a chapter, more a concise manual of biblical and common sense drawn from years of dealing with those hurt by the occult.

This point in the book is a pivotal point for one more reason. From now on, I take for granted that my readers will be mainly those who accept the Christian worldview. In short, I am now mainly writing for those who feel called to help those caught up with spiritual and occult problems.

I realise that by adding this solutions section, I am playing into the hands of my potential critics, especially those who cannot accept the reality of ritual abuse or the spiritual world.

Those who want to find flaws, for reasons of their own, may simply dismiss all that has gone before as 'what might be expected from an evangelical Christian who believes in the devil'. Obviously, I cannot hide who or what I am, and nor do I wish to do so. I press on hoping that at least the open-minded will use their integrity to evaluate the arguments so far presented. I press on simply because this solutions section is one of the major reasons for this book. It is no use stating problems without going on to possible solutions.

The battle

Amazingly, some of the following will be frontline spiritual research, even after 2,000 years of Christianity! It seems that we keep forgetting! Spiritual warfare is, for many, still largely a rousing hymn about soldiers standing up for Jesus, or a once-in-a-blue-moon rendition of the 'armour of God' chapter in Ephesians. Rather than wrestle with dark angels, we seem to be content to restrict the angelic to an appropriate season and merely pin up pretty pictures of cherubim to the accompaniment of 'Jingle Bells'.

God is today calling us back to the war front in a battle against dark forces which are so obviously ranged against the Christian church in the closing decade of this second millennium.

The logical way of providing practical, user-friendly strategies in this battle is to answer the questions Christians most often ask. Since my first book on the occult,[143] queries and pleas for help have come thick and fast via telephone, mail bag and training seminars. The following is designed to allow you to dip into any section or question when the need arises, or even as a general, easy-to-follow guide to the spiritual war front. Please treat it as you wish.

We start with a question that is increasingly being asked by those both inside and outside the church, as law and order begins to disintegrate under mounting pressure.

Q. *What can I say to those in the occult, or even in the church, who think the devil and evil spirits are inventions or myths?*

Some of the answer has already been given in Chapter 7 of this book.

Always state the whole case—subjective Christian reasons as well as the more objective evidence.

First of all, Christians believe in a personal devil because Jesus did. It would have been difficult to doubt a being who tried to brow-beat you while on a roller-coaster ride over temples and kingdoms (Matthew 4). The Christian logic is that if it's good enough for Jesus it's good enough for his followers.

Secondly, those who rule out the unholy spirit might as well rule out the Holy Spirit. Scripture has as much to say about one as the other. This, of course, is not to accept dualism—two sources of power. Scripture always stresses that the unholy spirit is a created being, originally the right-hand aid of the one supreme power, now in rebellion.

Thirdly, there is the testimony of previous generations and millions of Christians. Why should a comparative handful of modern sceptics in the last century, who seem to know little of God, change our minds?

Fourthly, it makes sense of life as it is: a God who delegates some of his power to his right-hand angel, who then makes an unsuccessful bid for the Number One position. On losing, the angel is cast down from heaven and promptly carries on the fight on God's other scene of operation—planet earth.

This last argument introduces us to the more objective, philosophical reasons for the existence of a personal devil.

Fifthly, everything in the world has a positive and negative; a good side and a bad side. Electricity can kill or warm. Weather can freeze us or fry us. Is it not therefore reasonable to expect a

good and bad use of spiritual power; a right and a wrong understanding of it?

Sixthly, the law of cause and effect points to an intelligence
behind evil. Everything in the world has a cause. When you see
a planned programme of evil it is right to look for an evil personality. Hitler produced World War Two; General Galtieri, the
Falklands Campaign; Saddam Hussein, the Gulf War.

There is reasonable evidence to suggest that there is a design
behind the world's evil, and therefore a personality. Look at the
facts of life:

The world: Forty warlords rule vast swathes of the world as I
write, and even so-called civilised Europe has its cities bomb-
blasted from Ulster across to Bosnia; all because of illogical,
stupid hatreds involving skin colours, beliefs, cultures and ter-
ritories.

A normal day in the life of our overcrowded, seemingly out-
of-control world will see 150,000 unborn babies aborted,
killing 500 mothers in the process. Of those who reach birth
today 25,000 will die within a year (many killed off because big
business insists on selling powdered milk to Third World vil-
lages that have only contaminated water). On this typical day
on our planet 350,000 adults will be infected with a sexually-
transmitted disease, but despite our ever-increasing ingenuity
at killing off ourselves, the overall population of the world will
increase by a quarter of a million.

The same population summit meeting of biologists, econo-
mists and mathematicians which produced the above statistics
also pointed out that the world's population had more than dou-
bled to 5.5 billion in just one lifetime. Zero population growth
'within the lifetime of our children' was the only way to save
the planet from ecological disaster and widespread starva-
tion.[144]

Modern sophisticated man gives all the classic signs of not
being in control of what he is and does. And if he isn't in con-

trol, then who is? This is an especially pertinent question when the sum of evil seems designed and programmed to wipe out the human race if it continues in its crazy lemming-like rush.

Family: Half the marriages of those under thirty-five collapse in the UK. The family, the building-block of our society since civilisation began, is disintegrating. Men and women who never plan for divorce when they marry nevertheless end up throwing each other away because they cannot control themselves. They seem to be governed by what is called 'the spirit of the age', and this spirit, far from being a faceless force, seems to have sufficient personality to be working to a plan. This can be seen especially in...

Society: Imagine for a moment that you fancy yourself as a world dictator. To win over society you need to make it weak, pliable, desperate, confused, and consequently more amenable to your management.

First and foremost, you would need to undermine its foundations, such as the family, law and order, morals and ethics. Ideally, you would aim to remove absolute rights and wrongs and encourage everybody to do what was right in his/her own eyes. A fair recipe for anarchy.

The best way of undermining the foundations of society would be to get the members to tear up its constitution, and for much of the world, that means the planet's best-seller, the Bible.

You would need to get society's intelligentsia to spread rumours that the biblical backbone of modern civilisation was after all nothing more than mere myth or legend; get people to talk about it being full of contradictions, even though there were none; get them to ignore it in daily life, especially in the legislative assembly; get them to make judgements on what will work, or what will win votes, rather than on what is right or wrong.

This is precisely what has happened in Western civilisation, and it is difficult to look back on the last 200 years of disintegration without getting the impression that it was planned. And if designed, then who is the designer? The story of a devil out to wreck mankind and keep us away from God suddenly seems quite plausible.

There are two final pieces of evidence to be considered in the argument for the existence of a personal devil.

Seventhly, the testimony of the survivors.

'Satan I've seen, heard, followed. Satan I know. Now show me your Jesus!'

This has been the challenge of many coming out of the occult and satanism. Many have experienced the power of Satan and it occasionally produces the logic: 'If an unholy spirit exists then maybe it's worth looking for the opposite.'

Just as there are millions who can testify to experiencing a real Holy Spirit as they come into a personal, living relationship with Jesus, there are also an increasing number who can testify to the reality of an unholy spirit.

When you see the effects of the devil in people's lives, lingering doubts about the existence of an evil personality disappear. When you see occult victims released from their obvious bondages, the doubts fly out of the window.

Finally, the incredible explosion of occult evil, even among the highly educated.

Amazingly, the majority in the occult and satanism are intelligent people who have been won over from a sceptical world. Take the average satanist in England. According to a national occult survey,[145] a third of satanists have university degrees, 80% are men with an average age of thirty-three, and a further quarter of the sample have had some form of further education. To reach the status of occult adept (master) is the equivalent of a four-year honours degree course at university.

People in the professions—teachers, lawyers and even theological students—do not follow something that is mere imagination or myth. There is a power which they tap into.

Bearing all the above evidence in mind, it is not unreasonable to believe that this power has a personality—just as the Bible says. We continue with the most frequently asked question—and the hardest to answer!

Q. *How do you tell the difference between a spiritual problem and a mental problem?*

With great difficulty!

Discernment in spiritual realms, as with diagnosis in the medical arena, involves both logic and inspiration, or 'technical knowledge' as well as 'charism', to use Dr Kurt Koch's definitions.[146]

In certain Christian circles, discernment is equated with a general spiritual feeling, or hearing the inner voice of the Holy Spirit. At the risk of being branded a heretic, let me state in bold letters: **This is the last thing you should rely on!**

Discernment is not so much a gamble of feelings, more a rational exercise in listening and learning. To be sure, I have known the Holy Spirit give direct words of knowledge about a person's spiritual predicament. And yes, there have been times when inner promptings have been proved right by subsequent revelations. However, just as medical doctors identify physical ailments with down-to-earth diagnostic techniques rather than inner hunches, so it should be for Christian healers in discerning spiritual problems.

My own golden rule in questionable cases is to advise the person I am helping to have a medical check-up with a GP. This in fact happens in many cases because, sooner or later, most spiritual problems work their way into the physical and psychological areas. I find that most of those who come for help do not take offence at this suggestion when I explain that spiritual problems often have physical, emotional and psychological side-effects.

Here are the steps of diagnosis which will help you:

(a) Listen. Ears are the counsellor's most effective tool. Don't be too eager to write out "prescriptions" before hearing the complaint in full.

(b) Take notes. Jesus asked a father how long his son had suffered (Mark 9:21). If Jesus took the trouble to discover background facts, how much more should we. The Holy Spirit needs you and me to have all the relevant information for discernment to be accurate: full name and address, family circumstances, upbringing and background, church links, involvement in occult areas, health history (especially any hints of mental illness, depression, etc), sexual orientation and views, present/past medication, worries, sleep pattern, employment or lack of it, and relevant history of close family.

You need permission to jot down details, and if this is not possible, commit the facts to memory and note them as soon as possible after your chat.

(c) Watch for the classic red-light signs of mental disturbance:

* Hearing voices which nobody else hears.
* Disorders in sleep/weight/appetite.
* Believing things that are obviously untrue or unusual.
* Extreme emotional upset.
* Speaking off the point.

Just a word of caution at this point: I have ministered to people who heard voices, had various disorders and believed things that I found extremely hard to accept. They were also suffering from extreme emotional upset. They were in fact the first two cases of ritual abuse that I dealt with. I have to confess that I saw the classic signs and jumped to the conclusion that both women were emotionally and psychologically ill. It was not until my third case of ritual abuse that I was prepared to accept that there may be an alternative diagnosis. Also, the above points are only 'red lights' to make us stop and think. They do not automatically mean that the person we are helping is 'round the bend'. It may just be that he/she is on one of life's normal, if zany, detours.

One last point in this section. Preacher and medic Dr Martyn Lloyd-Jones maintained that the demonised generally kept quiet and wanted solutions, while the mentally ill nearly always wanted him to be quiet so that they could start talking. And when they did talk, their disturbed minds always took the conversation onto a different wavelength, regardless of what had gone before.

(d) Watch for possible pointers to spiritual disturbance. These are less measurable than those for mental illness or trauma and, therefore, less objective and reliable.

* Acting out of character, but sanely and with logic.
* An impression of another personality battling with, or subduing, the normal one.
* Reactive to sacred things, such as the name of Jesus, the church, the cross, the blood of Christ.
* Speaking with, and behaving in, an apathetic monotone.

Those who minister in this area often find the demonised are apparently oppressed and overshadowed, as though their personalities have lost a dimension and been drained of colour. This can sometimes be accompanied by psychosomatic-type complaints, such as asthma and rashes.

One telephone call stands out by way of illustration. For three years I and others had ministered to Laura from Yorkshire. She was a weekly 'blood donor' to a group of satanists. Whenever we talked, whether face-to-face or on the telephone, a constant wheeze of breath accompanied our conversation. One day the phone rang, I picked it up and heard: 'Hi, Kevin. It's me! It's happened!' I recognised Laura's voice immediately—minus the wheezing exertion.

'I can tell!' I shouted back into the receiver. 'You're healed. What happened?' She laughed like a little girl and explained that she had spent a week away with some former Christian missionaries and deliverance had taken place.

Incidentally, if you are dealing with victims of ritual abuse who behave as though they are overshadowed or oppressed, it could be that they are dissociating. Victims who have gone through appalling trauma in ritual abuse learn to dissociate and even invent another 'environment' in which to exist. Dissociation can later easily become an automatic escape whenever life becomes difficult.

Having noted the main features of mental and spiritual problems, you will see that differentiating between the two is no easy matter. What can be said of spiritual problems can almost always be said of mental illness, and vice versa. This hopefully will reinforce the point that the Christian carer should never work alone, and referral to a GP while keeping a watching spiritual brief is often the safest.

Q. *How can non-Christian doctors and psychiatrists help cure spiritual problems?*

First, the layman is not competent to determine what is solely a spiritual problem. In America, a counsellor would have a malpractice suit slapped on him if things went wrong. This is now beginning to happen in this country.

Secondly, as we have already noted, spiritual problems very often have emotional and psychological side-effects, and these have to be dealt with, often with drugs and psychiatric counselling. In this situation, a local Christian fellowship is there for extra support and comfort.

Thirdly, when the mind bends or snaps—to put it crudely—

a mental 'plaster of Paris' is often needed to aid healing. Christian counselling and prayer will have as much effect on the broken mind as they do on a broken leg. Yes, miracles do happen, but God generally cures through the doctors and drugs he has already provided.

Fourthly, it has to be admitted that one of the best ways of helping people is to accept them for who they are, love them without strings, encourage them back towards self-determination, and help them establish worthwhile short- and long-term goals.

Now it has been established in various tests that those who are spiritually and mentally ill, and the traumatised, will often find the above treatment far more beneficial than all the mind drugs put together. The Christian healer does have a crucial role—so long as he/she does not go it alone.

Q. *I feel out of my depth. Surely ministry to occult victims is a specialist task and not for me in the local church?*

Yes, it is for you! It has to be. Consider the facts.

There has been an explosion of interest and involvement in the occult and satanism. The number of victims is proportionately increasing, but the number of so-called Christian specialists remains constant. The vast majority of those involved in ministry to occult victims have suffered burn-out. The local Christian church must take this ministry seriously while there is still time.

Each local church group or network needs to have people recognised in the counselling ministry, especially to those in the occult. In the Church of England each diocese has its team of advisors, and there are similar schemes in other denominations. They are usually more than happy to help local church teams to come to terms with this area of counselling.

We need above all to remember that no one ministry should be elevated or treated in any special way in the body of Christ. All are equally vital (1 Corinthians 12). Later, in Ephesians 4, it is stressed that some are called to be apostles, prophets, teachers and some are called to be pastors and evangelists, and deliverance can fall into either of these latter categories. The deliverance ministry may be different from that of, say, an elder, church warden or Sunday school teacher. But only in function. Not in status. All ministries are on the same level—just as important as each other—before God.

Q. *But how am I to cope? How can I work in this area?*

By the power and authority of Jesus Christ.

Fact one: Jesus Christ sent out his followers (Luke 9 and 10, for instance) telling them to teach and heal, and to deliver people from demons. They came back leaping for joy because the power Jesus gave them worked.

Fact two: By the time of the early church, spiritual deliverance appeared to be so normal that it rated only occasional passing references. For example, Philip in Acts 8:6–7 sends demons scurrying for cover as a matter of course in a normal evangelistic ministry. Maybe we should rename our present missionary endeavours 'the Decade of Evangelism and Deliverance'. Maybe our present evangelism merely tickles the demons into laughter rather than sending them scuttling for safety.

Fact three: Jesus promised that whatever his followers bound and loosed on earth would likewise have been done in heaven (Matthew 16:19). We only need to seek the kingdom's plan to learn what God's will is in any given situation. We then have a responsibility to exercise spiritual authority in Jesus' name, mainly as his church, but I believe this is also available to the individual Christian.

Fact four: Jesus commanded that all he taught (the preaching, healing, deliverance, everything) should be passed on to new disciples—you and I (see the Great Commission—Matthew 28:20).

Fact five: The same Holy Spirit who helped the apostles and

the early church is with us today. The same power! The same
authority! The same task! In a similarly pagan world!

If you are still in doubt...

Fact six: Jesus on the cross of Calvary and the resurrection
totally devastated and destroyed the pitiful power play of the
devil. The evil forces were, and are, completely routed and in
retreat (1 John 3:8; Colossians 1:13; Luke 10:17–18 and many
more such texts).

If only we Christians realised what power and authority we
have as representatives of the King of kings, we might even do
what the first disciples did.

Q. *OK! So Christians have authority. But what do I do about
it? How do I deliver those who have been in the occult?*

I believe there are five main practical forms of deliverance. But
first some practical DOs and DON'Ts:

DON'T go solo—even Jesus sent out his disciples in pairs
(Luke 10:1f). The dabbling do-gooder who goes it alone without help and support can be a menace to himself and those
he/she seeks to help.

DO go in prayer—you are not wrestling with flesh and
blood. Spiritual battles need spiritual power.

DON'T overpower those you are helping and *DO* be sensitive, even as the Holy Spirit is who comes as a dove. The
slightest hint of force will only convince an occultist that
he/she is about to step out of the frying pan into the fire. Certainly be encouraging, and let the occult victim set the pace,
though you will realise with experience that gentle persuasion
is sometimes necessary when the demons within the victim do
not want to co-operate.

DON'T minister if the occult victim is under the influence of
drink or drugs. Give support and care, but action should wait
for an oasis of sobriety.

DON'T manufacture demons. Investigate all normal explanations before turning to the occult. In some cases you may need to go no further than the straightforward common sense of referring a person to their GP.

One over-charismatic lady was experiencing 'funny sensations' and 'prickly touches', and consequently believed that evil spirits were trying to invade. It turned out that she was 'overdosing' on iron! The normal course of iron tablets during her first pregnancy was proving too much for her naturally-rich blood.

DO remember that we can be affected by three forces:

(a) The world: 'Do not conform any longer to the pattern of this world, but be transformed by the renewing of your mind' (Romans 12:2).

(b) The flesh: 'Watch and pray so that you will not fall into temptation. The spirit is willing, but the body [flesh] is weak' (Matthew 26:41).

(c) The devil: 'Be self-controlled and alert. Your enemy the devil prowls around like a roaring lion looking for someone to devour' (1 Peter 5:8).

Emphasise any one of these to the exclusion of the others and you can be in big trouble.

DON'T assume that a person is demonised because he or she has dabbled with a ouija board or even been in a coven. Remember that people can dabble in Christianity and remain completely detached from the Holy Spirit. The same can happen in the occult, even though the devil is no gentleman. People's natural resistance can be a great protection.

Tammy, for example, was brought up in the ritual abuse practices of generational satanism. It was only when she attended her first sex lessons at secondary school that she realised that what Dad and various uncles had been doing to her for years was not normal in other girls' homes. She became so angry that she began to hit out at 'everything in pants'. Such was her venom that she was expelled from school, sent to several borstals, then women's prisons and eventually to Moss Side (now Ashworth) Hospital for the Criminally Insane in Liverpool. Eventually, through the help of her Christian solicitor, she was released into the community in her early twenties. All went well until the satanists of her childhood found out where she was living. It was then that Tammy came to a 'safehouse' which my wife and I were then operating for victims of satanism. The following year, she quietly and beautifully gave her life to the Lord.

The point of this story is that Tammy needed little deliverance ministry—mainly because she had been protected by her strenuous, pig-headed refusal to go on submitting to the satanic way.

DO use natural anger. Controlled righteous anger can be a useful force in our ministry. Jesus himself showed a stern seething hatred of evil when he commanded evil spirits to be quiet and to come out of the man in the synagogue (Mark 1:25). Controlled anger can also encourage the deliverer, and even the one being delivered. Note the word 'controlled'. We want the demons, not the affected person, to flee.

Now to five practical steps of the deliverance ministry:

1. The classic hands-on approach

Know your authority and quietly but firmly exercise it. Lay hands on, or around, the victim and tell the demons to go to hell, or consign them to Jesus to be dealt with.

Think of a traffic policeman as you consider this form of deliverance. He calmly and professionally signals for you to pull over and he parks in front of you. He takes his time radioing in, slowly gets out of the patrol car, turns to walk back and reaches casually for his notebook. He has not shouted. He has not stamped his foot or shaken his fist at you. Yet you are shaking on the inside.

'Did you know, sir, that you were doing forty-five in a thirty mile per hour zone?' You open your mouth to reply, and a stammer stumbles out.

A policeman wears his authority as clearly as his uniform. In the spiritual world, you and I as the King's representatives have an even greater authority; the same authority that Jesus had; that same authority that made the demons scream out, 'What do you want with us, Jesus of Nazareth?' (Mark 1:24). Incidentally, note that it is the demons which do the shouting and screaming, not those who deliver, nor the person being delivered.

2. *Deliverance through love*

While the hands-on approach can often be a useful last step in deliverance, the opening of the arms begins it.

Accepting, caring, listening and giving in authentic Christian fellowship can actually be a means of deliverance itself. A no-strings-attached fellowship can be an infusion of real life for an occultist who has been programmed to use people or be used. It hardly needs to be stated that we must be wary of using occult survivors as scalps or prizes in our churches. They should be accepted for who they are, not what they have been.

Warts and all need to be accepted. In the case of occult abuse victims, this can involve odd sexual orientations, swearing and drinking and chain-smoking, out-of-control eating habits—in fact, any or all of the human appetites can be distorted to one degree or another. People needing care come out of a world-view which knows little of self-discipline, control and moderation. Loving, accepting Christian fellowship is needed rather than constant condemnation. What they don't need is pressures and controls imposed from the outside. That will come all in good time when the Holy Spirit grows his own fruit on the inside.

Here, there is personal sadness for me. I have known people come out of the occult only to return because of unbending, strait-laced fellowships that found them too messy.

3. Deliverance through truth

There are few things in life which can compare to the golden moments of illumination as the first glimmer of truth dawns in the previously-dull eyes of an occult survivor.

The truth really does set people free, as Jesus promised (John 8:32). It delivers them into the light of understanding as the devil is put in his place, and God is elevated to his. The good news of the Holy Spirit and the demise of the unholy spirit from Creation to Revelation by way of Calvary acts as a razor-sharp sword on the bonds of those emerging from the occult.

There is one truth that is particularly important to apply to those coming out of the occult. It is the truth of diminished responsibility.

Guilt can be quite devastating for occult survivors—especially for those who have gone on to abuse others. But how much have they been sinned against and how much are they the sinners? They often need help in apportioning blame. In nearly all cases, they blame themselves too much.

Hannah still haunts my memories as one who could never come to terms with her guilt. As a Christian, she could accept that Christ had forgiven her her sins, but she found she was unable to forgive herself.

'I can't stand the screams of the children in my head!' she used to cry. She had been abused in group satanic practices and then she had been forced to do the same to other children, including one of her own. Such was her anguish and so deep was her consequent depression, that she took a massive overdose of pills one morning and died seventeen days later in our local hospital.

Diminished responsibility is also true for those born into occult traditions, which is happening more and more in modern times. We need to remember the logic of spiritual inheritance in which blessings and curses do not stop at one generation. It is a foundational truth, enshrined in the Ten Commandments, that the sins of the fathers will affect the children to the third and fourth generations. So often this cause-and-effect chain rattles through centuries: incest begetting incest, hatred giving birth to hatred, and so on. There is such a thing as sin being dyed in the bloodline of a family; ancestral sin that goes on breeding across at least three or four generations. Some forms of satanism, according to victims, thrive on passing on the belief system throughout the family's generations. It is regarded as honourable.

We need to be able to tell those born into the occult that their guilt is diminished because of family-inflicted abuse, and that there is a new family they can join, led by a forgiving Father who can break the power of ancestral sin.

Applying truth into darkened lives opens the way to the next method of deliverance, and possibly the best...

4. *Do-it-yourself deliverance*

This is the method I always encourage.

To be sure, I can lay hands on victims and exercise my God-given spiritual authority, but how much better that they come into a relationship with God and exercise the authority in their own lives.

It is far more powerful when victims themselves stand up to the devil and his forces and tell them where to go. It means that such self-rescued people have no ongoing need of the 'expert', for they can do it themselves with the power of the Holy Spirit. Obviously, Christian carers will still need to be around for encouragement and fellowship.

If victims choose not to deliver themselves, once they have become Christians, there is still need for some participation, if only at the confessional stage. Rejection of evil needs to be voiced and then carried through into action.

5. *Use of formal services*

Formal rituals of the church, such as baptism (if appropriate) and the Eucharist, times of confession and absolution and blessings can be more appropriate in some cases, especially where full-blown deliverance seems to be inappropriate. The baptism promises, incidentally, make a good structure for a do-it-yourself deliverance because of the promises to renounce evil and to follow Christ. There is also the official rite of exorcism which can be carried out. In my own Anglican church, this rite is to be performed only by permission of the diocesan bishop and with the help of his deliverance advisors. There are similar arrangements in other denominations—a sensible precaution after some disastrous exorcisms in the sixties and seventies.

We need to bear in mind that exorcism or even a full course of deliverance counselling and ministry may prove too much for those who only require, say, a prayer of blessing. John Richards in his Grove Booklet on the ministry[147] illustrates this with the following story:

A patient comes to a doctor for a pain in her toe. The doctor refers her to a consultant whom, somewhile later, he meets in the street.
'Did you cure my patient with a painful toe?' inquires the doctor.
'Yes. I guarantee she'll never ever suffer pain from it again.'
'That's remarkable! What did you do?'
'I arranged for her leg to be amputated!'

A small, quiet service is sometimes all that is required. Hopefully, it hardly needs to be said that we should avoid dead ritual—an automatic recitation of prayers and ceremonies. I have an uncomfortable feeling that this is what the seven sons of Sceva did in Acts 19. The sons of a Jewish chief priest tried to drive out an evil spirit with the formula: 'In the name of Jesus, whom Paul preaches, I command you to come out.' It was obvious they did not know Jesus personally, and the evil spirit took advantage of this and beat them up.

Finally, on deliverance, a suitable combination of some or all of the above may be appropriate. Ministry often needs to be fitted to people's needs.

Q. *Why should I risk being beaten up like the sons of Sceva?*

The question is not often put like this. More often it is a question of fear, mainly from those who give the devil too high a status. True, we should respect his power, as Jude 9 makes clear, but we need to recall that the power of Satan is limited.

Remember Morph, the tea-time plasticine television character who had us chuckling as he transformed himself into various comical shapes and situations? The devil is to God as Morph is to his creators. This is a powerful illustration for those coming out of the occult and who fear the devil. Get them to model Bluetac into a figure and then have them squash it, and then get them to identify the flattened figure as Satan in God's hands.

Remember that Satan can do nothing without permission (that's the truth emerging from the downfall of Job, and also 1 Corinthians 10:13 and Revelation 20:2,7). There is nothing that the devil can do to us without God's permission. And if God does allow something to happen, then it will be for our good in the long run (that's the truth of texts like Romans 8:28). Whichever way, we win! Even Satan knows that his authority is not his own, but is derived from somebody greater (Luke 4:6).

Remember that Satan is hopelessly outnumbered. In Revelation 12 there is the implication that two-thirds of the angels are left to oppose the rebellious one-third (fallen angelic stars), and whether or not we take this as literal, this text and many others makes it abundantly clear that the devil is just not strong enough to take on the might of heaven.

Remember also that it is highly unlikely to be the might of the devil ranged against you or me. We ordinary mortals probably rate the attention of hell's minions, while the devil takes on the likes of archbishops and popes! An over-simplistic picture, true. But it is probably a lot nearer the truth than fearing a personal satanic visitation. Satan is a created being with limited knowledge, and is limited to being in one place at one time, unlike the Creator who is all-knowing and everywhere (cf Isaiah 40:12-17; 57:15f).

Q. *What if those we are trying to help don't want to be delivered?*

Respect their wishes.

Remember the free-will, gentleman's approach of God towards us. If the Lord will not gatecrash a person's life, neither should we.

This doubly applies to those we believe to be affected by evil spirits as a result of their occult involvement. Some Christians, from the best possible motives, try to coerce, pressurise or manipulate those they care about to submit to some form of ministry. It is the worst thing they can do.

What if they actually succeed in ridding a person of an evil spirit without his/her full involvement, faith and co-operation? Jesus implies that the person will end up seven times worse than the original state if they are then left unprotected (Matthew 12:43f).

It is true that Jesus did release the demonised on rare occasions without a sign of faith (ie, Mark 1:21 and 5:1f), but what is safe for Jesus with his often special knowledge is not necessarily acceptable for his more limited followers. In fact, I have come to believe that it is unwise to use the deliverance ministry with anybody but Christians and those in the process of conversion. I have stated this at numerous seminars, and it has invariably led to the next question…

Q. *Are you trying to tell us that Christians, filled with the Holy*

Spirit, can be possessed by evil spirits?

NO. But the Bible does say that Christians can be demonised.

We get the word 'possession' from the Authorised Version of the Bible. Later versions have also struggled to convey the original sense, using phrases or words such as 'people with 'demoniacs' (Revised Standard Version), and 'demon-possessed' (New International Version). The original Greek means 'to be as a demon' or 'to be demonised', neither of which means much to the average Englishman. The latter, even though it sounds like a do-it-yourself car waxing product, is the most accurate, and the one I prefer to use.

Many in the deliverance ministry shy away from the word 'possession' because it does not truly reflect the whole range of states which are encountered. There are victims who are simply oppressed (affected by external evil forces) and those who are obsessed (who merely stand at the doorways of the occult and are addicted by some form of it). To be 'demonised'—to be affected by a demon—covers the whole range of states.

Now people—be they Christians filled with the Holy Spirit, or non-Christians—can certainly be affected by evil forces.

James instructed his Christian readers to resist the devil. Why? So that he will flee and not affect them (4:7).

Paul told the Ephesians to put on the whole armour of God. Why? To protect them from the flaming arrows of the evil one (6:16).

John and Paul insisted that the early church tested the spirits. Why? Because Christians could be influenced by wrong ones (1 John 4; 1 Corinthians 12:10).

Timothy is warned to steer clear of believers who follow deceiving spirits and things taught by demons (1 Timothy 4:1–2), and Paul again warns the Corinthians that they can be 'participants with demons' (1 Corinthians 10:20).

Christians who let the sun go down on their anger can even

give the devil a foothold in their lives (Ephesians 4:26f). Scripture plainly teaches that Holy Spirit-filled Christians can be affected by unholy spirits. If this is so, why have Christians traditionally opposed the idea of being demonised?

It stems from the faulty view of what we are like. We tend to see ourselves as receptacles into which the Holy Spirit is poured, and of course certain pictures in Scripture tend to reinforce this concept (ie, 'be filled with the Spirit', Ephesians 5:18). However, this view when taken literally belittles not only ourselves but the Holy Spirit.

God's Spirit is the dynamic Third Person of the Trinity, not some stagnant inert liquid waiting to be shaken and stirred and poured into us. And you and I are not leaky mugs which have to be kept topped-up. Your being, like mine, is incredibly complex, a living drama of body, mind and spirit. Forget being a container. See yourself as you are in reality—three strands of body, mind and spirit constantly interacting and affecting each other, rather like three intertwining lines on the screen of a hospital bedside monitor (see diagram).

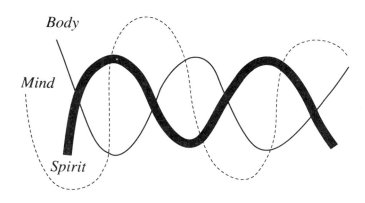

Even this is too static a picture, but at least it removes the concept of us being receptacles. At conversion, the Holy Spirit comes to create a new spirit within (Ezekiel 11:19; 2 Corinthians 5:17), and our new Spirit-filled spirit begins to radiate outwards to renew our minds and our bodies (Romans 12:2f).

Is it not now easier to visualise how we can be demonised; how we can be impacted from any direction by the flaming arrows of the evil one? And they can strike from any and all directions, and at any unprotected parts of body, mind or spirit. No wonder Paul implores us to put on the whole armour of God. We need it.

Having got thus far, indulge me a little further while I mount a small hobby-horse.

Why is the deliverance ministry not a central part of local church life? Why do normal Western Christians shuffle with embarrassment when demons and evil spirits crop up in conversation? Why, month-in, month-out, do I get Christians telephoning from the other end of the country in tears because their local church minister 'isn't into that sort of thing'? Why are we Westerners afraid to do anything more than paddle around in the shallows of Christianity? Could it be, could it possibly be, that the Evangelical, Bible-believing wing of the Christian church finds this part of God's word too much to swallow? Would they prefer to run their pens through these verses about demons, evil spirits and deliverance? And could it possibly be that this is why the Christian church in the West is so lily-livered, weak-kneed and so totally ineffective, because it would rather fight flesh-and-blood battles than take on the powers of darkness?

If you are still with me, thank you. Every writer should be allowed at least one explosion per book.

Q. *I feel like I want to take my mind out and wash it clean after listening to some occult problems. What do you suggest?*

Carers themselves need to be cared for, especially those involved in occult counselling. They need good supervision in the local church situation and a chance to debrief after particularly difficult cases. Help is needed in the management of feelings, especially in abuse counselling when a carer's own hidden fears or suppressed memories can be resurrected. Carers can too easily feel attacked themselves.

Good management structures for carers are needed, and this can be tackled in two organised ways...

1. A special deliverance task group

The advantages of this are that there is more support for, and from, each other, and a greater sharing of expertise and information. The main disadvantage is that the team becomes isolated from other carers in the church. It can also lead to secrecy ('We can't talk about it outside the team'), and élitism ('Why are they so special? I have difficult cases as well'). Also deliverance counsellors can find it difficult to escape the rarified atmosphere of their special group and can become dominated by it.

2. Deliverance alongside other counselling tasks

The advantages of this are a greater link with reality and a more normal perspective on life and the ministry. The main disadvantage is that one occult victim can often claim a pair of carers for months, and this may lead to resentment among other counsellors who have to carry the rest of the church load. It can also mean increasing guilt for carers who feel that they should be taking a greater share of the burdens. This leads to increased chances of burn-out.

Good management of a caring team can go a long way to dealing with the disadvantages.

Q. *What can we do in our local situation to warn people, especially youngsters, about the dangers of the occult?*

Managers at high street newsagents are often unaware that they are promoting the occult through magazines, comics, horoscopes and tarot cards. Some can be sympathetic, especially if you present yourself as a polite and sensitive concerned parent; better still, a group of concerned parents. If the newsagent is a manager and will not listen, make representations to the head office.

Proposals for occult shops can be tackled via the letters column in local newspapers, local planning departments and councillors. Access and Barclaycard have been known to withdraw their accounts from suspect shops. Occult fayres, occult content in libraries and schools and the media can all be tackled on similar lines. Full details can be gleaned from *Action Agenda*, an Evangelical Alliance leaflet (see penultimate question in this chapter for address).

I have come to believe that the best way forward is through warfare in prayer. The early church combined both the practical and spiritual approaches with great effect. The apostles were always ready to act against the devil within the church (Ananias and Sapphira who had been filled by Satan—5:3), and also against those outside (Simon the Sorcerer—8:10f), but they were men and women of prayer and power doing many wonders and signs (2:43, etc).

We had a small encouragement in this area when an occult shop opened in my last parish. I immediately suspected the owner's motives, for there was little call for the occult in the small East Lancashire town in which we were ministering at the time, and the opening followed close on the heels of quite a few television and radio appearances in which I had criticised the occult. I discussed what should be done with my church wardens and leaders, and we came to the conclusion that publicity was just what the occult shop owners were after. We decided instead to continue with our regular Tuesday afternoon leaders' prayer meetings just round the corner from the new shop. Four months later it closed its doors for the last time. I'm not usually an outwardly 'Praise the Lord!' type—but *Praise the Lord*!

Q. *How do I reach Aunty Flo? She won't do a thing without touching wood, reading her tea-leaves and then double-checking with her daily stars.*

Our biggest enemy until recently was spiritual apathy. Relatives, friends and workmates were totally indifferent to the inner life as they grasped continually for material happiness. Talking of spiritual matters in this atmosphere was rather like broadcasting on Radio Three while everybody was tuned in to all the other stations.

Not so today! Increasing numbers are turning away from the emptiness of possessions and tuning in to the illusory vibrations of a hundred-and-one gurus. And it presents Christians with a thousand-and-one chances in what I call 'question-mark evangelism'. The truth, and especially Christianity, has nothing to fear from questions. The more questions asked, the nearer the seeker will be to the truth. On the other hand, the occult and satanism have much to fear and everything to lose when placed under the microscope.

We can begin to encourage our aunts, uncles and assortment of relations to think more deeply about their beliefs. We need, with gentleness, to stretch their thinking until their ideas begin to be tested at the seams. We must, however, do it with love. We want to win friends and relatives rather than the arguments.

Some useful questions to those in the occult might be:

1. Is it wise to allow our lives to be guided by lumps of matter whizzing through space? Can a setting Venus really put the dampers on our love lives? The moon may affect earth's tides, but can it influence our personalities? And even if was true that massive lumps of matter could affect us and our personalities,

wouldn't the bulk of, say, our fathers at conception or the rotundity of the midwife at birth have far greater gravitational effect on us?

2. Does Aunty Flo not get a little anxious to think that her fortunes are at the ebb and flo of a drained blob of damp tea-leaves?

More seriously...

3. If everything is one interconnected whole, where did it come from? Who or what caused it to exist? Who or what designed it? Can some mindless cosmic force really be responsible for the mind-challenging complexity of a snowflake, a living cell or our ability to understand this question? What massive intelligence lies behind the intellect of Plato, Newton and Einstein? Is it intelligent merely to state that intelligence comes from a big bang via a blob of primordial mud at the bottom of some stagnant pond? And even if we did come from a big bang, who or what created the laws of physics and mathematics which governed it?

4. If we are really part of the cosmic force, and therefore part of God, who or what are we going to worship? Or what happens if we make up our own gods to suit our own whims and fancies? Every society that has ever existed has had its gods. Can we now accept that we are gods? Are we to worship ourselves? If so, are we worth it? And if we think so now, will we think so when an accident puts us flat on our backs with only ourselves to answer our prayers?

5. And can we really play fair in a world which has no external referee and no rule book? Won't anarchy ensue if everybody plays according to their own private laws—or passions? What if one person's weekend pleasure is a round of golf, while another's involves ritually abusing children? Who's to say which is acceptable? Can there be right and wrong? And if there is no almighty external referee, what right has one part of society to dictate to another part what it should or shouldn't do?

I remember putting a similar question to Christos outside Pole Cottage after he told me that a satanist followed his own path regardless of others. He eventually accepted that he and other satanists could only live this way so long as everybody else stuck to the rules. It would be impossible if everybody decided to live their own way without considering anyone else.

Do remember that your quiet, loving questions may be all that is standing between your friend and hell.

Q. *How do we begin to cope with a survivor of satanism or ritual abuse?*

This is increasingly being asked, especially by church ministers who discover that they are into something which seems way over their heads. Though I have ministered to many in this area, it seemed best to go to one of the best. Maureen Davies of Beacon Foundation takes up the answer in the next chapter.

Q. *Where can I get more help?*

The Beacon Foundation: 3 Grosvenor Avenue, Rhyl, Clwyd, North Wales LL18 4HA, for help in coping with victims of occult and satanic abuse.

Reachout Trust: Alpha Place, Garth Road, Morden, Surrey SM4 4LX for useful literature and practical help on all cults and the occult.

Christian Response to the Occult: Selsden House, 212-22O Addington Road, South Croydon, Surrey CR2 8LD, for well-produced leaflets and expertise.

Cult Information Centre, BCM Cults, London WC1 N3X, advice and literature on those caught in cults and the occult.

ACT – Association of Christian Teachers: 2 Romeland Hill, St Albans, Hertfordshire AL3 4ET. Excellent alternative resources for schools at Hallowe'en, plus schools leaflets.

Evangelical Alliance: Whitefield House, 186 Kennington Park Road, London SE11 4BT. Various action leaflets on occult, including *Doorways to Danger* and others.

Christians in Caring Professions: 175 Wokingham Road, Reading RG6 1LT (tel. 0734 660515), for excellent counselling courses and education.

London Healing Mission: 20 Dawson Place, London W2 4TJ, for ministry and counselling.

13

Caring for Survivors

by Maureen Davies, Director of the Beacon Foundation

In the late eighties, I was asked to help a teenager who had been arrested for desecrating a church. Through it, I came to realise how easy it was for youngsters to be brainwashed and caught up in black magic. The court placed the teenager in care and away from the occult recruiters for his own safety, yet the root problems—his emotional needs, coping without a father and his craving for supernatural power—were ignored.

Since then, there have been many enquiries for help from those related to teenagers who have become involved in witch-craft and satanism. Some have become psychologically dis-turbed, and a few have attempted suicide.

In 1988, I was introduced to my first case of ritual child abuse, and since then there have been many more, referred by social services, the medical profession and various voluntary organisations, including the church. We are now receiving enquiries from France, Germany, Norway, South Africa and America.

In 1991, we believed that it was right to set up a special trust, The Beacon Foundation, so that we could help professional carers to have a better understanding of the problems caused by involvement in the occult. Our task now includes monitoring the occult, researching how it damages the physical, emotional and mental development of those involved, keeping society informed of our findings, supporting victims and their families, and educating the church about the occult, especially ritual abuse.

The carers

Professional carers—psychologists, psychotherapists, social workers, vicars—can do only so much with ritual abuse survivors. Establishing them as free and mature members of society can take a team anything up to two years, and such a team needs far more than professionals can possibly give. It requires the constant active support of general carers, those who will befriend survivors, and provide them with that most precious of all ministries: a talk over a quiet cup of tea.

Carers almost choose themselves. They are the ones to whom the survivors find they can readily relate; those who can be trusted; who will listen without condemnation. To be a carer, you need to be prepared to deal with issues that can surface as a result of the developing relationship: anger at what you hear; frustration at the slow rate of improvement; powerlessness in the face of the abusing cult, and sexual fantasies or problems which can result from constant repetition of warped and perverted practices. The survivor can also experience sexual fantasies about the carer and, having shared them, will then watch to see how the carer will cope with them.

It is a demanding responsibility, and yet a great privilege. All carers with whom I have spoken have said that they are better people for having helped a ritual abuse victim, despite the hard work involved. The carer's role involves times of great joy, laughter and deep friendship, as well as tears and trauma. It will be in this relationship that the survivor will learn how to relate to others. She (for most are female[148]) will learn how to have an honest relationship, avoid lying, and come to know that she can share with people and still be safe. The carer's role is as important as the therapist's, for he/she often becomes a substitute parent, with the task of retraining a ritually abused person in all the social skills that the survivor has either never been taught, or which she has lost in the brainwashing practices within a cult. This reparenting generally takes place once the abused person moves out of the 'victim' pattern of behaviour, and begins to see herself in a more positive light—as a survivor.

We need to give space and time to those who have been severely abused and allow them to grieve and mourn, and to integrate into society at an appropriate pace. The journey into healing is a time when we are being given, and will become, 'a crown of beauty instead of ashes, the oil of gladness instead of mourning, and a garment of praise instead of a spirit of despair... oaks of righteousness, a planting of the Lord. They will rebuild the ancient ruins' (Isaiah 61:3–4).

We should not dare to speed up such a time as this when survivors are learning so much about themselves: self-worth, acceptance by others, their potential in Christ, forgiveness and (what is to them the incredible fact) the love of Jesus. Watching survivors blossom into life is as beautiful and precious as the water lily bud unfolding itself in the warmth of the morning sun. God promises through Isaiah that those who are bruised and broken will also be those whom he will choose to be the ones to rebuild, restore and renew.

Ritual abuse—a reminder

Before we go any further we need to remind ourselves of what ritual abuse is, and of the beliefs involved. A survivor is brainwashed with these beliefs, and they do not disbelieve them overnight.

Definition: 'Ritual abuse is repeated physical, emotional, mental and spiritual assaults combined with a systematised use of symbols, ceremonies and the use of evil, designed and orchestrated to attain harmful effects to turn the victims against their own selves, society and God' (Jerry Semandl, Chicago Police Officer).

The beliefs

Some beliefs common to most of the survivors we have dealt with are:

* Satan is god and he rules this earth with a highly-organised army of spiritual forces. Some have been taught that it is a privilege to serve him. Serious satanists meditate daily for instructions.
* Vows made to Satan are sealed in blood. They believe that death is the only way out. They renounce the Judeo-Christian God whom they are taught to believe died on Good Friday without a subsequent resurrection.
* They must obey Satan, for disobedience incurs punishment.
* Leaders and rituals are never to be questioned. The possibility of leaving is not on the agenda. If members leave there will be physical punishment or a campaign to break the rebel emotionally.
* Advancement is generally reserved for those who have a family history of obedience to Satan. Promotion can mean competing with friends for higher levels.
* Curses and spells play an important part. Other activities include violent torture, bestiality and sexual perversion.

Reprogramming

Brainwashed survivors of such a belief system need a great deal of loving re-education. Here are some examples of the positive truths which we need to present in order to help victims to become survivors:

* Affirm that they are loved; that it is OK to be loved and to love. They will have been told that no one cares and that they cannot love.
* Affirm the positive parts of their lives as well as dealing with the negative past.
* Encourage them to take some control of their healing, to counter the lie that they do not have choices. At times they can exhibit a learned helplessness from their abuse.
* Encourage them to think and feel; that sharing opinions is healthy; that differences of opinion do not mean the end of relationships.
* Teach them to have fun (even playing on swings, having an ice-cream).
* Show them that 'in Christ' *all* of us stand to inherit *all* the blessings as a child of the 'First Born'. It is not like satanism and the old covenant where only the eldest gains.

The above is part of the process called Exit Counselling, helping to deprogram the brainwashed. The victims need to know that they have been lied to, and that there is a way out, given time. Fear is a tremendous tool which the perpetrators use on their victims: fear of leaving the group, fear of talking, fear of breaking vows, fear of revenge, fear of blackmail. There are several others. Many hours of love and affirmation are needed to break through these barriers. Perhaps the greatest fear is reserved for those who suffer abuse within the family. Ending the abuse means breaking with the family—and the terror of being alone.

The main input from a carer must be the constant love and encouragement aimed at developing the self-worth and ego of the survivor. Some who have been ritually abused think that they have no right to have friends; to have people care for them; to ask for help, or ask Jesus Christ to come into their lives. It is a beautiful moment when survivors not only ask Jesus for help, but believe that they have every right to do so.

Guidelines for carers

1. Supervision and accountability to a team leader

This is needed to safeguard the well-being of each member of the team, to promote professionalism, and to assist each other with some of the often alarming things that emerge in the healing process.

2. Establishing boundaries for all concerned

The survivors especially need to know the boundaries, for they often do not realise when they are pushing beyond the normal limits of relationships. This is usually because they become overwhelmed with the attention they are receiving and, fearing that it might soon end, try to claim as much as possible. This, of course, is the very thing that usually wrecks the friendship. The carer's responsibility is to pace the relationship so that it does not break. The survivor, like the normal child, is actually grateful to know the limits.

Boundaries need to be set on time spent together and on the telephone. Boundaries are also needed within the team so that each member knows who is doing what and when. It is good to bring in outsiders occasionally to share the emotional strain, even if they only invite the survivor for a cup of tea.

3. Breaking with the past

There will often be an uncertain time to begin with, and you may not know for sure whether or not the abused person has left the cult, coven or whatever. Patience is needed. Sometimes the victim will need time as she is talked through the consequences and advantages of a complete break.

4. Reparenting and re-education about the non-occult world

This is especially relevant for those abused in domestic situations. They have to relearn, or even learn for the first time, how to relate to, and with, parents, other members of the family and the world at large.

5. Difficulties of dissociation

All of us dissociate at one time or another, and in its mildest form we know it as day-dreaming.

Ritual abuse victims quickly learn to dissociate during the horrors which they endure as a way of retaining their sanity. They create what for them becomes another reality; an escape world where they can shelter until the hurt has gone away. Over the years and through repetition, dissociation can become second nature, and the slightest stresses of life can bring on such a state.

The carer does not need to understand this condition totally to be able to help. Some of the causes of dissociation include the recalling of painful incidents, strong emotions attached to the abuse, or it could simply be that the auto-hypnosis has degenerated into a lazy habit that has become difficult to control. When a survivor goes 'off', the carer can ask, 'Where are you?'—gently offering reassurance while recalling the abused person back. The therapist has the responsibility to treat the problem, and the carer's simple task is to bring the dissociation to the attention of the abused person—the first step in managing the habit.

6. Dealing with flashbacks

The mind might learn to exclude unpleasant reality through dissociation, but there is often no escape from flashbacks which can rip to shreds even the most powerful of mental defences. Flashbacks occur when a person's violent past breaks vividly into the present, and the survivor finds herself reliving the abuse all over again. When this happens, she is no longer in the here-and-now, but trapped once again in abuse, and it is distressing not only for the abused, but also the support team. In a full-blown flashback the victim can sometimes assume the positions in which she was abused.

The therapist will be required to teach the survivor how to stay 'grounded' in the present, and carers can be an encouraging support at this time. Some therapy centres spend months teaching survivors how to manage this area before real treatment of the flashbacks begins.

Helping survivors stay in the here-and-now involves identifying the causes of flashbacks, encouraging self-discipline and using various grounding techniques, such as simply being there to affirm that the survivor's flashback is a fantasy; that it is not really happening, and that she is safe and surrounded by people who care. There is also the need to identify the triggers which switched on the flashback. These can be normal, everyday words, pictures and smells which the perpetrators have 'programmed in' to the abused person to make them co-operate. A check needs to be kept of these triggers and they will need to be discussed and dealt with at the right time.

7. Dealing with voices

Most ritual abuse survivors have voices which represent various aspects of their fractured personalities.

One way of understanding what is going on in the survivor's head is to ask her to separate the voices, and these generally fall into three categories: injured child, adult and dark side.

The injured child knows that she has had horrendous things done to her, but cannot come to terms with them. The adult may be cut off from the pain, or not prepared to look at its source. Some think that life is too busy for this introspection, while others know that they cannot avoid investigating because the pain is interfering too much with the present. The dark side may want things to remain as they are, possibly to avoid giving up addictive behaviours and other similar reasons. Very often, a carer needs to ask the survivor to identify in which 'state' she is responding. There are also other less dominant voices, such as those belonging to the perpetrator or other victims.

8. Suicidal feelings

The source of these feelings may be the 'adult' facet of the survivor nearing breaking point, though usually it is more likely to be the 'injured child' who just wants to escape the pain. In this case, a carer can encourage the 'adult' to 'look after' the child within. This split in the survivor's personality is often one of the most difficult areas for the normal whole, well-integrated person to understand.

Suicide can also be induced by the self-hatred which the survivors feel because of what they themselves have done, or been forced to do. Some believe that suicide is the only solution, having been programmed to believe that death is the only way out.

Dates can be very significant for those who are suicidal. Particularly important are the times of the year when rituals took place, survivors' birthdays, or an occult festival. At these times survivors may feel urges to return to the cult, despite the suffering of the past.

I have only attempted to cover some of the problems encountered in helping ritual abuse survivors. They sound enormous and are at times overwhelming, and you may now see the great need for carers to take care of themselves and pace their relationships. I hope the enormity of the problem does not put you off, for if we do not help these people, then who will? We can do this task with the grace of God, and there is much that survivors can teach us and give to us.

The greatest input needed for healing is love. Are you prepared to be a channel of God's love for these folk? For them it can often be a matter of life and death. For us as carers, it can be a rich journey in which there is a deeper, more satisfying walk with God as we care for those he loves.

14
Veronica's Story

Part Two of this book has been about providing some solutions to the problems of satanism and the occult, as set out in Part One. Perhaps the best solution of all is provided by Veronica, the lass from Liverpool who featured in the early chapters. Here are her own words to make sense of her escape from the occult...

As one who has spent a long time searching for spiritual truth and meaning; delving deep into the supernatural and dabbling in other spiritual areas, I finally *know* I have arrived!

I've at last found the answers I spent more than a decade looking for, and with those answers has come a security that striving for material goods, relationships and life could never provide. I've found a life in Jesus Christ; a living relationship with God, and a sound knowledge of exactly where I'm going when I die.

My story is too long and complicated to relay in detail, and for the present I am not legally free to write everything down, but I would like to share a little of how God changed me.

I feel an affinity with the Wiccans, the New Agers and occultists, not because I'm interested in their philosophies now, but because I was once one of their number. Like them, I was spiritually hungry, searching, fickle—chasing various 'paths' or traditions for an enlightenment that somehow always eluded me, even though I didn't realise it at the time.

My pagan gods had various names. They were picturesque personifications of 'forces' I didn't understand. Some in the occult said that they merely represented various aspects of the individual's own unconscious, but I *knew* these were external forces. A great many inexplicable events occurred in my life, coincidences maybe, but to be honest they scared the living daylights out of me. They certainly didn't give me any peace, happiness or security.

I can honestly say that my depression, my change of personality, my inner fears and insecurities were directly and indirectly attributable to playing with psychic powers I didn't understand. This was not obvious at the time, but in retrospect it is. Slowly, indiscernibly, subtly, the occult took over many aspects of my life, and while it didn't exactly ruin it completely, it took away much of its quality. That time of searching in the supernatural was the most lonely and confusing of my life—a dark time.

When, in 1987, I came across 'King's Kids', singing and praising Jesus, I wanted what they had—their exuberant joy, their indefinable yet almost tangible spirituality—and so I asked God to let his Son Jesus into my life, and with tears of joy I welcomed him in. My life changed! Gone were the old gods, the psychic abilities, the beliefs of my past. In their place came joy, peace and a relationship with God, with his power in every aspect of my life. Who needed rituals, spells and magic when the Creator of the universe, the great I AM, was at work in my life? More importantly came a knowledge that the Lord had come to earth as a man and had personally suffered and shed his blood for me. People may scoff when they look at that from a purely academic standpoint—no one can accept it by intellect alone—but when you know it's the truth spiritually; when you've accepted it spiritually, it's the most profound, beautiful, powerful experience of your life and *the* most important.

As Kevin knows, I went through many traumas, and yes, I slipped back into my old system of beliefs for a while, but God gently and lovingly guided me back to him, and with his guidance I was able to withstand the most awful and unbelievable traumas, especially when the children were taken from me.

I don't want to sound like just another bigotted, fanatical evangelist to those in the occult. Many in the occult have felt judged and hounded by them. I used to feel judged and hounded too. I don't want to preach in that way or to be in any way patronising. All I want to do is share with them my experiences, which affected me profoundly, and show them not the god of dead churchianity, but the living, very real God who is able to meet with them where they are today, in whatever situation, and offer them so much more than the old gods ever could.

This God can be met through Jesus Christ, simply through trust and faith; by allowing him lordship over your life.

If just one person comes to know Jesus because of this short testimony, then everything I've been through will have been worth it.

End notes

1. Earl Spencer, the brother of the Princess of Wales, said in his maiden speech in the House of Lords that devil worship had taken place on his estate at Althorpe, near Northampton. Lord Spencer was speaking in favour of landowners opening up their property to the public despite the occasional weird useage. Following his speech, he explained that his gamekeepers had seen regular evidence of 'things left on the ground' and that devil worship had been a 'common complaint' in the previous three years. *Daily Telegraph*, (17th June, 1993).

2. Figure taken from 'The Extent and Nature of Organised and Ritual Abuse' compiled by Professor Jean La Fontaine, emeritus professor of social anthropology at the London School of Economics.

3. There is support for this seemingly general figure of a million involved in various paths of the occult. Active involvement in the orthodox occult paths (witchcraft, Chaos Magic, satanism, etc), according to guides like the Occult Census, published by the Sorcerers' Apprentice, would be in the low hundreds of thousands. To these need to be added those involved in the New Age, the psychic, the paranormal, not to mention those addicted to their daily horoscopes and astrological charts. Mar-

ket research tells newspaper editors that with seven out of ten women reading their stars, they would be unwise to leave them out of their papers and magazines. Actually, my million seems rather a conservative figure.

4. Report of the Metropolitan Police Force's investigation into satanic ritual abuse, completed February 1994. See also note 2 above.

5. Valerie Sinason (ed.) *Treating Survivors of Satanist Abuse* (Routledge, 1994).

6. I have appeared with Beth Gurevitch on a number of television discussion programmes, such as Kilroy, and she has consistently maintained that she is a white witch using her powers for good. However, I'm not too sure how this ties in with the televised occasion Beth stuck pins in an effigy of MP Geoffrey Dickens, after he had criticised witchcraft and its influence in the House of Commons. Hansard (14th April 1988).

7. The occult has traditionally been divided into the Right-Hand Path (those using magic for so-called white, good purposes) and the Left Hand Path of the black magicians.

8. This distinction between Lesser and Greater Black Magic appears in the Temple of Set. See Chapter 9.

9. A description of the two women who masterminded the appalling torture and burning alive of teenager Suzanne Cooper. *Today* (18th December 1993).

10. 666 is used in forms of the occult as the mark of Satan, and is borrowed from the Bible, where it is recorded as the mark or number of the beast (Revelation 13).

11. Statistics of missing children published by The Children's Society (24th October 1988). Of the 532 children who came to the society's London safe house in a two-year period 98% said that they had been sexually abused at some point in their lives.

12. Names and addresses of these groups are given at the end of Chapter 12.

13. *The Tales – The Truths* leaflet in author's possession. Copies can be obtained from The Sorcerer's Apprentice, 6/8 Burley Lodge Road, Leeds.

14. The SAFF 'Truth' leaflet was not exactly the whole truth. For instance, in the Hazel Paul case, 'The Truth' article claimed that 'the use of the ouija board was incidental to the abuses...perpetrated by people who were not part of the occult group, who never claimed to be occultists...' The SAFF article, however, was selective in its defence. It made no reference to the boy's occult-related testimony, and avoided mentioning the boy's devil testimony and Paul's psychic powers.

'The Truth' article then went on to the Newell case, admitting that the accused 'was indeed an occult fan—but he was not a satanist...' and that 'the other significant parts of the case which Reachout & the Reverend Logan did not want you to hear is that on appeal the judges said that the court has been misled and should have considered a plea of self-defence'. (This was partly true. When I originally published this case I had no knowledge of an appeal.) The article added, 'Newell's flatmate was his best friend. There was never any evidence to suggest that he had been killed on an altar, or for ritualistic purposes. Newell was a beginner occultist...whatever drove Newell to murder his flatmate it was not occult involvement.'

It is difficult to share the writer's certainty surrounded with the mountain of occult paraphernalia in the case. Again, the SAFF article is not the whole truth and is selective and misleading. It failed to accept that there was more than sufficient evidence, as we have noted, to suggest occult involvement and even a ritual element in the killing.

15. A good example is the audio-cassette tape entitled *The Chaosphere* which I purchased from the Sorcerer's Apprentice Astonishing Books in Leeds. It includes the following:

Chaos magic is dangerous, awesome, full of potential and therefore mysterious…it has an ultra-sinister aspect to it…anyone can jump into the cauldron of chaos and discover powerful magic, and the only rules are those imposed upon oneself by one's own courage…We specify our desire, open up our subjective will to render our reality malleable, and then throw ourselves on the mercy of the gods. This then is the danger of chaos magic. We prepare to sacrifice our identity and intellect in order to interface with the void. We give ourselves up to death.

16.   Kevin Logan, *Paganism and the Occult* (Kingsway, 1988).

17.   A motorist without documents is given an HO/RT/1 form which requires presentation of driving documents at a nominated police station within seven days.

18.   The five-pointed star is variously known as the pentacle, pentagram or the pentalpha. It is the sign used by most occult groups in one way or another. Pagans, witches or followers of the white magic path use the symbol with one point upwards. Satanists and black magicians reverse the symbol with two points uppermost, often forming the two goat ears of Baphomet. The five-pointed star became the occult symbol because it represents many of the esoteric and occult qualities.

19.   Necromancy is about divining the past, the future, or the spirit world's will by calling back to 'life' the spirit of a corpse in order to persuade it to give the required information.

20.   Asmodeus, according to the Apochrypha, is a tormentor of Tobias' betrothed. According to Fred Gettings' *Encyclopedia of the Occult*, Asmodeus is associated 'with power of the deadly sin of lechery' and is 'the demon pledged to plot against newly-weds and to estrange the hearts of virgins and waste away their hearts'.

21.   Judge Denis Clark, at Liverpool Crown Court, as he jailed a satanist for child rape.

22.   On the occasions when I use first names only in this book,

they are pseudonyms. These are used to protect the people involved or, as in the case of Veronica, for legal reasons. Her children are still wards of court at the time of writing, though she hopes this will have changed by publication.

23. Professor Jean La Fontaine, associated with Inform, based at the London School of Economics, was commissioned by the Department of Health to produce a report on organised and ritual abuse. This was restricted to abuse involving children only.

24. The European Network for Backlash Research (ENBAR) was set up at the end of the eighties. ENBAR exists to support those helping ritual abuse victims who then face the backlash of a disbelieving society. By 'backlash' they mean a 'powerful, efficient and unjust reaction to an initial just action which was meant to address an obvious injustice (i.e. an organised denunciation of those who seek to redress the injustices of abuse)'— ENBAR, F. Clockstraat 167, 9665BJ, Oude Pekela, The Netherlands.

25. In establishing this definition of ritual abuse, I have paid particular attention to the well-researched and respected offerings of the following: Finkelhor, Meyer and Burns, *Nursery Crimes and Sexual Abuse in Day Care* (Saga Publications, 1988); the British NSPCC, and the Ritual Abuse Task Force, LA County Commissioners for Women.

26. *Social Work Today*, 26th October 1989 and *Community Care—The Independent Voice of Social Work* (14th December 1989).

27. NSPCC figures from their press release accompanying their 1990 annual report (12th March).

28. See note 23 above.

29. Andrew Boyd, *Blasphemous Rumours—Is Satanic Ritual Abuse Fact or Fantasy? An Investigation* (Fount), p 7.

30. Tim Tate, *Children of the Devil—Ritual abuse and satanic crime* (Methuen).

31. Christian Psychiatrists' Conference at the Medical Associ-

ation, London, in 1988.

32. Quoted by Andrew Boyd, *Blasphemous Rumours* (Fount), p 12.

33. *Ibid*, p 15.

34. *Ibid*, p 24.

35. *The Independent on Sunday* (1st May 1994). Report on child abuse conference at Leeds University.

36. Mr Jim Baker quoted in *The Independent on Sunday*, (18th March 1990), p 5.

37. *Daily Mail* (19th October 1990), P 9.

38. *Ibid*.

39. *Daily Mail* (25th April 1994), p 12.

40. New Age style business is the latest rage in industry and commerce, as I have outlined in my last book, *Close Encounters with the New Age* (Kingsway). In Skelmersdale, a few miles from where I live in Lancashire, there is a large industrial estate owned and run by TM adherents, and all workers are encouraged to take two twenty-minute breaks for tea and meditation.

41. The technical word for one-ism is monism—the belief that all is one. It is similar to pantheism which agrees that all is one, but adds that that one is God.

42. Francis King, quoted from the introduction to S.L. Mac-Gregor Mathers et al, *Astral Projection, Ritual Magic and Alchemy* (Golden Dawn).

43. *Ibid*, p 36.

44. John Symonds, *The Great Beast* (Purnell), p 15.

45. *Ibid*, p 17.

46. *Ibid*.

47. *Ibid*.

48. *Ibid*, p 18.

49. Israel Regardie, *The Eye in the Triangle, an Interpretation of Aleister Crowley* (New Falcon Publications), back cover.

50. John Symonds, *The Great Beast* (Purnell), p 18.

51. *Ibid.*

52. Aleister Crowley's privately-printed book was *Alceldam*.

53. Quoted by Israel Regardie on back cover of *The Eye in the Triangle* (New Falcon Publications).

54. Aleister Crowley, *Magic*, p 268.

55. R.G.Torrens, *The Golden Dawn*, p 11. Torrens also points out that many of the early masonic lodges were 'orientated to the setting or rising sun' and 'others were aligned to receive the light from certain stars'. This was done to 'focus light from one of the heavenly bodies, direct and unpolluted, into the Holy of Holies over the heads of the assembled congregation'. He adds that 'anyone who has knowledge of masonic working in higher degrees, will mark a part of one ceremony which maintains a record of this in its rituals'. The occult roots of free-masonry and its incompatibility with Christianity are tackled in my book *Paganism and the Occult* (Kingsway).

56. I have in my possession the OTO's own list of administrative and governmental offices and official bodies as of 15th May 1987. I also have its organisation flow chart.

57. Rosicrucians were so named after fifteenth-century Christian Rosenkreuz who ran various teaching groups studying an esoteric mix of Christianity and the occult. It became a society teaching that man needed to be regenerated by a process of spiritualisation. For several generations, the Rosicrucians went underground, but their tradition of hermetics and alchemy later came to light in the works of Boehme and Fludd. Some suggest that Rosicrucianism was a source of the first freemasons in the seventeenth century.

58. In this case, magic is spelled with a 'k' at the end, which is the way many in the occult choose to spell the word. I have kept to the normal spelling throughout this book, except where I quote occultists' own written words.

59. Quoted by Andrew Boyd in *Blasphemous Rumours* (Fount), pp 124-5.

60. Fran Skinner, *Witchcraft for Non-witches*, (a privately-circulated booklet in author's possession), penultimate page.

61. Quote from Robin Skelton in Andrew Boyd, *Blasphemous Rumours* (Fount), p 129.

62. The full quote is taken from *The Practice of Witchcraft Today*, Robert Hale, 1988, pp 21, 33.

63. *Chaosphere* tape (see note 15).

64. *Black Mass* quote from *Children at Play* leaflet (Evangelical Alliance), p 3.

65. *Ibid.*

66. *Summer Witches*, quoted by Sarah Strickland and Rosie Waterhouse, *The Independent on Sunday*, (28th October 1990), p 3.

67. *Ibid.*

68. All-in-Vayne, *Pagan News* (August 1989).

69. Baroness Cox quoted in the *Church of England Newspaper*, 26th June 1992).

70. *Daily Telegraph* letters to the editor 1st August 1992.

71. A Department of Education survey carried out among 2,500 children attending fifty Avon schools showed that children, on average, watched 22.08 hours of television each week—only three hours less than school time. Following a different survey, the Independent Television Commission in July 1993 ordered programme-makers to cut down on the violence. Another survey by the International Coalition Against Violent Entertainment revealed that British children see 80,000 horror scenes before they are eighteen years old. Lund University in Malmo, Sweden, conducted a ten-year study and concluded that children who often watch violent television or videos are more aggressive and delinquent, and have more problems concentrating than other children. It showed that there was a direct correlation between emotional disturbance and intensive television and video viewing.

72. H. Gleitman, *Psychology* (third edition) chp 3.

73. Pat Pulling, Rosemary Loyacono and Patrick Dempsey, *Dungeons and Dragons* (BADD, PO Box 5513, Richmond, VA 23220) outlines the 'negative aspects and direction of the D & D books'. Several associated suicides are quoted.

'The games teaches the philosophies of witchcraft and Satan worship,' explain the authors.

The following are taken from the *Advanced Dungeons & Dragons Player's Handbook*:

To animate the dead: requires a drop of blood, a piece of human flesh...(p46).

Tlaloc (Rain God). At each full moon, a priest Tlaloc sacrifices a child or baby...after which the priest cooks and eats them...(p35)

Kali (Black Earth Mother). Her worship requires sacrifices or blood, and even an occasional human sacrifice (p75).

There are pages of similar quotes. Pat Pulling and her co-writers add:

> We find examples of young people being sucked into a vortex of undesirable real-life behaviour. We find young people stepping into their characters becoming one with this same D & D character [sic]. We find emotional involvement at a high level while playing the game particularly when one's character is killed. Depression often results; sometimes violence—sometimes murder—sometimes suicide—sometimes mental problems. We have now witnessed libraries and educators taking on a great liability by allowing the game to become part of the curriculum or programme. Who will take the blame for a suicide or mental problems evolving from the game? Who will be liable? Who is willing to lose a son or daughter?

74. Abbadon interview in the *Daily Star* (25th July 1990).

75. Psychic poll conducted by *The Times* in 1980.

76. Poll conducted by Southampton University and published on an ITV programme, *Is Anyone There?* on Hallowe'en 1987.

77. Quote from an occultist called Gregory, as he charts his path to satanism.

78. William Roache, *Ken & Me* (Simon & Shuster, 1993) pp 184-185.

79. 'Me and My God', *Sunday Telegraph* column, (15th August 1993).

80. Comment on the Knights Templar by Schwarz and Empey in their book *Satanism*.

81. Don Bothwell, the biological adviser on the Lindow investigation, stated: 'It is as if almost all the methods of killing someone had been encapsulated in this one individual.' He suggested it was 'the sort of violence which perhaps made sense as part of a complex ritual'.

82. Ted Schwarz and Duane Empey, *Satanism – Is your family safe?* (Zondervan), p 30.

83. *Ibid*, p 33.

84. *Ibid*, pp 36-37.

85. Christos, Order of Nine Angles' *Fenrir* magazine.

86. Taken from special 'Hostia' edition of *Fenrir* in author's possession.

87. Anton Szandor LaVey, leader of the Church of Satan, in his book *The Devil Worshippers*.

88. Personal letter from the Church of Satan in author's possession.

89. Walpurgisnacht on 30th April-1st May is one of several occult and satanic festivals throughout the year. It is also known as Beltane (Bel's fire welcoming the sun and new life). Other festivals are based on the solstices (summer, 20th June; winter, 21st December) and equinoxes (spring, 20th March; autumn, 22nd September). The most well-known festival is Samhain (Hallowe'en) on 31st October, when the spirits of the dead are believed to emerge from their places of burial. Other celebrations will take place on New Year's Day, Candlemas (2nd February), Good Friday (in mockery), Lammas Day (1st

August) plus members' own birthdays.

90. Michael A. Aquino, *The Church of Satan* (Temple of Set), third edition, p 309.

91. Blanche Barton, *The Church of Satan* (Hell's Kitchen Productions Inc), p 35.

92. *Ibid*, p 10.

93. *Ibid*.

94. *Ibid*.

95. *Ibid*, p 11.

96. Anton LaVey, *The Satanic Bible* (Avon Books), p 25.

97. Attributed to Anton LaVey, *The Devil Worshippers* in Tim Tate, *Children for the Devil* (Methuen), p 140.

98. Blanche Barton, *The Church of Satan* (Hell's Kitchen Productions Inc), p 23.

99. *The Crystal Tablet of Set* (Temple of Set), XXII edition.

100. *Pretenders to the Throne* (Church of Satan).

101. *The Crystal Tablet of Set* (Temple of Set), XXII edition, p 45.

102. *General Information and Admission Policy* leaflet (Temple of Set), p 6.

103. *Ibid*.

104. Michael A. Aquino, quoted in *Gnosis Magazine* (1989).

105. *Nox*, the occult magazine of the Abyss, explaining the satanic order of the Werewolf.

106. Dr Jim Philips claimed this 10% figure during a BBC1 *Panorama* programme in July 1993, entitled 'In Satan's Name'.

107. Peter Brierley (ed), *UK Christian Handbook* (Marc Europe and the Bible Society), 1994 edition, p 281.

108. *The Occult Census* (Sorcerer's Apprentice, Leeds).

109. Anton LaVey, *The Devil's Notebook* (Feral House).

110. Interview with Anton LaVey, *The Observer* (8th August 1993).

111. Article by Dr Bogart in occult magazine in author's possession.

112. *Ibid.*

113. 'A Brief Explanatory Letter to Enquirers', sent out to all who enquire about the order.

114. *News of the World*, 17th July, 1994.

115. Temple of Olympus advertisement in the occult magazine *Insight* (issue no. 38), copy in author's possession.

116. Article by Jackie McKeown, *Croydon Advertiser* (26th January 1990).

117. See note 15.

118. *Fenrir* (vol. III, no. 1), copy in author's possession.

119. See note 15.

120. *Nox* magazine (January 1990), vol 2, no. 3.

121. Gerald Suster interviewed in *Pagan News* (July 1989), p 121.

122. Genesis P-Orridge interviewed in occult magazine in author's possession concerning his and his wife's, 'motivations and philosophical imperatives for their tattooing, piercing and scarification explorations'.

123. *News of the World* article and interview (24th January 1993).

124. Pandora Corey on the *South Bank Show* (1992).

125. As explained in Vampyre Society leaflet (issued from 9 Edgar Road, South Croydon, Surrey CR2 ONJ).

126. Ganymede literature in author's possession.

127. Derry Mainwaring Knight trial, Maidstone Crown Court (April 1986).

128. Beacon Foundation, 3 Grosvenor Avenue, Rhyl, North Wales.

129. There are several well-established women's groups of freemasons in Britain. These are run independently of the main Grand Lodge in London.

130. Pamela Sue Hudson, licensed psychiatric worker and child therapist with the Mental Health Institute, Mendocino County, Northern California.

131. Andrew Boyd, *Blasphemous Rumours* (Fount), back cover.

132. Books dealing with the ritual abuse issue include: Tim Tate, *Children for the Devil* (Methuen); Andrew Boyd, *Blasphemous Rumours* (Fount); James T. Richardson, Joel Best, David G. Bromley *The Satanism Scare* (New York: Aldine de Gruyter); Dianne Core with Fred Harrison, *Chasing Satan* (London: Gunter Books). Health Department report by Jean La Fontaine entitled 'The Extent and Nature of Organised and Ritual Abuse' (HMSO).

133. One of the themes pursued in James T. Richardson, Joel Best, David G. Bromley, *The Satanism Scare* (New York: Aldine de Gruyter).

134. C. Hall and G. Lindzey in *Theories of Personality* (USA: Wiley, 1957) investigate fully Jung's famous 'collective unconscious' theory, seeing it as a storehouse of latent memory traces inherited from man's ancestral past. Patricia Hughes asks whether humanity is predisposed to revive memories of past experiences if Jung is correct and there is a collective unconscious. Alternatively, is it 'the therapists and clients who are reporting these cases responding to the Jungian concept of the collective unconscious'?

135. Herod's slaughter of the innocents (Matthew 2). The worship of Molech, a god of the Ammonites, involved the sacrifice of children in fire (Leviticus 18:21; 20:2-5; 2 Kings 23:10).

136. Aleister Crowley, *Magic in Theory and Practice*, Chapter 12 entitled 'Of the Bloody Sacrifice'. Taken from special 'Hostia' edition of *Fenrir*, published by the Order of Nine Angles, in author's possession.

137. Pamela Sue Hudson, a licensed psychiatric social worker and child therapist with the Mental Health Institute, Mendocino County, Northern California, as quoted by Tim Tate, *Children for the Devil* (Methuen), p 1.

138. Valerie Sinason (ed), *Treating Survivors of Satanist Abuse (Routledge)*.

139. Patricia Anne Campbell Hughes, 'An Exploration of Satanic Ritual Abuse: Past & Present', University College of North Wales, September 1993 (dissertation submitted in partial fulfilment of requirement for the degree of MEd).

140. J.G. Friesen, *Uncovering the Mystery of MPD* (USA: Here's Life Publishers, 1991).

141. J. La Fontaine, *Child Sexual Abuse* (Polity Press, 1990), and H. Giarretto, NSPCC Conference, London, 1990.

142. Perhaps a note of caution should be added at this point. Certainly, agencies should work together as far as possible, but it now seems that some of them have been pursuing this new hand-in-glove approach so vigorously that they are losing their traditional critical framework of checks and balances, according to the *Sunday Telegraph* on 8th May 1994. This is apparently one of the findings of Christine Hallett of Stirling University, who studied cases undertaken by several units involving police and social workers in joint enquiries.

143. Kevin Logan, *Paganism and the Occult* (Kingsway, 1988).

144. Statistics produced in a fifteen-page statement by Professor Roger Short at the Population Summit, New Delhi, October 1993.

145. The Occult Census, published by the Sorcerer's Apprentice, Leeds.

146. Dr Kurt Koch in *Christian Counselling and Occultism* (W. Germany: Evangelization Publishers, 1972).

147. John Richards, *Exorcism, Deliverance and Healing, Some Pastoral Guidelines* (Grove Booklets on Ministry and Worship, (no.44), p 15.

148. While it is true that the Occult Survey revealed that 80% of satanists were men, more than 90% of the victims are female. The women claim that they have been sucked into satanism as victims rather than members.

Index